MW01143869

To Carter.

You radiate light, joy and laughter wherever you go.
I Love You.

Note for Librarians: A cataloguing record for this book is available from Library and Archives Canada at www.collectionscanada.ca/amicus/index-e.html
ISBN 1-4120-7382-0

Printed in Victoria, BC, Canada. Printed on paper with minimum 30% recycled fibre. Trafford's print shop runs on "green energy" from solar, wind and other environmentally-friendly power sources.

TRAFFORD PUBLISHING™
Offices in Canada, USA, Ireland and UK

This book was published *on-demand* in cooperation with Trafford Publishing. On-demand publishing is a unique process and service of making a book available for retail sale to the public taking advantage of on-demand manufacturing and Internet marketing. On-demand publishing includes promotions, retail sales, manufacturing, order fulfilment, accounting and collecting royalties on behalf of the author.

Book sales for North America and international:
Trafford Publishing, 6E–2333 Government St.,
Victoria, BC V8T 4P4 CANADA
phone 250 383 6864 (toll-free 1 888 232 4444)
fax 250 383 6804; email to orders@trafford.com
Book sales in Europe:
Trafford Publishing (UK) Limited, 9 Park End Street, 2nd Floor
Oxford, UK OX1 1HH UNITED KINGDOM
phone 44 (0)1865 722 113 (local rate 0845 230 9601)
facsimile 44 (0)1865 722 868; info.uk@trafford.com
Order online at:
trafford.com/05-2277

10 9 8 7 6 5

Prologue

"Either you believe or you don't. If you do, then you know what to do and now you must do it. If you don't, then you must keep searching."

This quote is at the end of this book. It is perhaps the most profound realization that you will come to in this Life.

There is a way to Live Life. The way is not special or complicated. In fact, it is *so* simple and self-evident that we overlook it.

Coming to realize that there is a way to Live Life is very important. Once you come to that realization, you must then search for the way. Once you have found the way, you must then walk it.

This book is intended to help you in your search for the way. I believe that I have found the way and I would like to share with you my "way to the way." If you have already found your way, perhaps this book will help you to stay on it.

I have not yet fully realized my enlightenment. I have yet a long way to go. In fact, the only difference between me now and the me I used to be is simply this; I used to be lost, but now I know the way. That may not sound very profound, but it is.

I am now really just beginning my Spiritual journey. The time up 'till now has been spent trying to find the starting line. I am now done walking in circles. I now know where to go and how to get there. I have perhaps taken only the first few steps on my journey, but the few steps that I have taken following the way have been more fulfilling than ten thousand that I took when I was lost.

I encourage you to read this book with conviction. If you believe that what you are reading is just a bunch of useless "new age mumbo jumbo" or the same old "Spiritual gobbly goop," you've heard before, *it will be.* If you believe that what you are reading will open your mind and profoundly change your Life for the better, *it will.*

I encourage you to read this book slowly and deliberately. Read it once a week for at least three weeks in a row and continue to read it until you "get it," (come on now, it's short). You will know when you "get it."

You will find that the more you read *Conversations With Myself*, more and more of its truth will be revealed to you. You will find new revelations about yourself and about Reality the more you read it. Quite often it takes just one certain phrase to strike home, and like a bolt of lightning your mind will be opened to a truth previously obscured.

There is a way to Live Life. The part of you that tells you there isn't is the part of you that keeps you from finding the way. It is my genuine hope that this book will help you to find the way.

CONVERSATIONS WITH MYSELF:
A Most Common Dialogue.

Me: Hello.

Myself: Hello, how are you?

Me: Fine, how are you?

Myself: I'm well, thank you. Do you mind if I ask you a few more questions?

Me: I suppose not. Go ahead.

Myself: Who are you?

Me: I'm Roy Dopson.

Myself: Where are you?

Me: I'm at home.

Myself: What are you?

Me: I'm a human being.

Myself: What time is it?

Me: It's 2:33 p.m.

Myself: Why are you?

Me: Why am I what?

Myself: Just that, *why* are you?

Me: …I don't know.

Myself: Things were going along pretty smooth until I asked you that last question, hey?

Me: Ya, for some reason my mind just kind of stalled when you asked me why I was. I could tell you how I was, who I was, where I was, what I was, and what time it was, but I couldn't come up with a reason for *why* I was. Why is that?

Myself: You couldn't come up with *a* reason for why you exist because *All* is the reason for why you exist. All that you are and All that you are not is the reason why you are. All that you do and All that you do not do is the reason why you are. The reason why we exist is existence itself. The division of existence does not provide us with a more precise description of the reason. The lowest common denominator of reason is existence. It doesn't matter if we are talking about one thing that exists or if we are talking about everything that exists. It doesn't matter if we are talking about doing one thing or if we are talking about doing everything. The reason why we exist is to experience existence.

Me: Well that was more than I was ready for! I'm more confused now than I was before I asked the question.

Myself: Being confused is a good thing, it means that you are thinking beyond your usual parameters. Thinking beyond your usual parameters is necessary in order to transcend to higher levels of Truth.

Me: Well, I don't think that I've "transcended to a higher level of Truth." Can you maybe simplify that answer a bit for me?

Myself: Okay, let me put it to you in another way. Asking why we exist is like playing a giant game of "Jeopardy" in which the universe is the answer and we are trying to come up with the right question. Let's say that you pick "All" for $500. The answer comes up "Eating a ham sandwich." You in turn guess the question to be "How to satisfy your hunger." But Alex tells you "No, I'm sorry, the question we were looking for is: "What is the reason for existence?" So you pick "All" (all of the categories are "All") again for $1000. This time the answer is "Pine tree." You quite confidently state the question to be "What comes from a pine cone." Unfortunately Alex says "No, the correct question is: "What is the reason for existence?" To your dismay every time you think that you have the correct question, Mr. Trebek informs you that it's not the one that he's looking for. The only question that seems to matter is "What is the reason for existence?" and everything is the answer!

We are the answer and all of our questions eventually must lead us back to ourselves. Until we realize that the answer is already with us we will keep asking questions.

Me: Okay, so if we are the answer, why do we ask why in the first place? Why all of this searching for something that we can't help but see? I can't accept that the meaning of life is to simply do everything that we are already doing. If everything that we do is the meaning of life then nothing I do can be wrong.

Myself: More or less.

Me: So I could beat the crap out of some old lady and steal her purse and that wouldn't be wrong?

Myself: You tell me. Do you feel as though it would be wrong?

Me: What kind of a person do you think I am? Of course it would be wrong!

Myself: Okay, on a "wrongness" scale of 1-10 how would you rate beating the crap out of some old lady and taking her purse?

Me: 10.

Myself: What about if you would have killed her? Wouldn't that be worse than just beating her up?

Me: Ya, I guess it would be worse if I killed her.

Myself: So if killing her would be worse than just beating her up, you'll have to re-think your original rating.

Me: Okay, so beating her up is a 9.5 then.

Myself: Oh, so now you're switching the scale from 1-10 to 100.

Me: Hey if you're going to keep changing the situation then I can change the rating system.

Myself: Fair enough. Now how about if you would have raped and tortured her before you killed her? How would you rate that?

Me: You're a real sicko, do you know that?

Myself: I'm just trying to make a point. How would you rate that on your scale of "wrongness?"

Me: 100.

Myself: So that act would be 100% wrong, there wouldn't be anything that could be done that would be more wrong? How about ordering the slaughter of 6,000,000 people?

Me: This is stupid! You can't judge how wrong something is. All of these actions have been 100% wrong. They're all wrong and there is no reason to rate how wrong they are.

Myself: First you changed the scale from 1-10 to 1-100 and now you're changing it to 1-2. Either an act is wrong, 2, or it is not wrong, 1.

Me: If you'd like, sure.

Myself: But didn't you just say that you couldn't judge how wrong something is?

Me: I'm not judging how wrong something is, I'm judging wrong from right.

Myself: What is the symbol for the judicial system?

Me: A blindfolded woman holding a scale.

Myself: That's because if you are going to judge something you must use a scale. There must be something to measure "wrongness" and/or "rightness" in increments so that the line between right and wrong can be distinguished. If you set a point between right and wrong, then whether you like to admit it or not you must constantly weigh your actions to see what they measure up to on the scale. This can be very draining.

As the actions changed, so did the increments on the scale. The more that you compared one act to another, the more complicated the weighing process became and the scale kept changing to adapt to the new standard. At first there were 10 units of measure on the scale and then that changed to 100 units as there became more acts to compare the original act to. Finally you became frustrated at how complicated the whole process was becoming and you constructed the simplest scale possible, the scale of either-or.

The whole process of separating rightwrong is quite complicated and leads to more confusion than clarity. A life lived trying to do right and trying not to do wrong turns out to be a life wasted. It's a wasted life because the energy used constantly *weighing* life could have been put into *living* life. In the end, labeling things as "right" or "wrong" isn't wrong, so much as it is unnecessary.

Me: So how do I stop weighing life and start living it? If I have no gauge by which to live, such as right and wrong, then what exactly should my focus be on?

Myself: "Focus" is a good word to use. Your focus should be on Life itself. Life is inherently perfectly balanced and any attempt at weighing it is ultimately futile. One may label acts as either "right" or "wrong" through whatever process deemed correct and then try to do all of the "right" things, but that's like cutting up a picture into a jigsaw puzzle and then trying to put all of the pieces back together. That may be a fine way to stay occupied, but the only bad part about it is that there is no end to the picture. At any given moment there are an infinite amount of "right" things to do in varying degrees of "rightness". This in turn means that there are an infinite amount of "wrong" things to do in varying degrees of "wrongness." How does one decide which is the correct path to take? What is the equation, the rule, the law, that encompasses every possible situation that arises in each person's Life?

Me: How about the Ten Commandments?

Myself: The Ten Commandments are the way in which the enlightened live their Lives, they're not the way in which to live Life in order to become enlightened.

Liberation is not a result of living your Life in accordance to the Ten Commandments. Living a life in accordance to the Ten Commandments is a result of being liberated.

A liberated person doesn't need to try to follow the Ten Commandments because he doesn't want anything other than what he already has. Lying, cheating, stealing, murdering, etc. all come about from wanting something other than what you already have. Wanting something other than what you already have is a result of your Life appearing to be unbalanced in some way. You then seek out this "something else" in an attempt to restore balance. The appearance of your Life being unbalanced is an illusion brought about by the belief that you are separate from everything else. The belief that you are separate from everything else comes from losing your focus on Reality.

Me: How do we lose our focus on Reality?

Myself: We want to share our experience of Reality with each other, and in order to do this we must separate the whole experience into individual experiences. We do this by using the five questions of "how", "who", "where", "what", and "when" that I asked you at the beginning of the book.

When we believe that the way in which we describe Reality in order to share our experience of It is actually the way It is, we have lost our focus on Reality. How, who, where, what and when Realty is, is *not* the way Reality is. How, who, where, what and when is the way in which we *describe* Reality.

Me: How *is* reality, then?

Myself: I can't really tell you.

Me: Why not?

Myself: Because if I told you how things are or what you should do, I would be starting the whole messy process that was mentioned above. The best I can do is share with you my experience and what I have learned from it.

Me: Okay, what *have* you learned from it?

Myself: Well, one of the major things that have helped me is the realization that our true nature is perfection. When God was finished creating All there is, He called It good. Everything *is* perfect; not everything *has* perfection. One cannot *possess* perfection. We can't go out and get it somehow because we already *are* perfect.

Once this knowledge is realized, one no longer has to question anything again because what would be the point of trying to instill order onto something that is already perfectly ordered? If there is nothing more to question then there is nothing left to do but experience; just take It all in. What is the animal used to symbolize wisdom?

Me: An owl.

Myself: Let's look at the qualities that an owl possesses that symbolize wisdom.

Me: Okay. Well, owls have huge eyes.

Myself: You hit the nail right on the head. Owls have incredible eyesight and those huge eyes help them to see even in the dark. They also have necks that can turn 180 degrees either way, so they are able to see a full 360 degrees all around them. Owls also sit for long periods of time without moving or making any noise, not drawing attention to themselves or disturbing anything.

Wisdom is the knowledge gained from seeing things as they are. The owl isn't wise because it knows the square root of 3,480,214 or because it can quote Shakespeare. The owl is wise because it sits quietly and sees All.

Me: If it's so wise, why does it still ask the question "who?"

Myself: Ha ha. Maybe it's not asking us "who" but telling us "who." Maybe it's telling us that it sees us for who we really are.

Me: Who really *are* we?

Myself: Well that's the question, isn't it? That's the search for the ultimate Truth.

The search to find ultimate Truth must ultimately be the search to find our True selves. The moment that we find our True selves is the moment we realize that *the experience is in the searching.* The converse also applies. The moment we realize that the experience is in the searching is the moment we find our True selves. This is the irony of being human. We are searching for something that cannot be found as long as we continue to search for it because it is the search itself that we are looking for. One does not have to look *for* something that is already there; one merely has to look *at* it. Looking for a Truth that is outside of ourselves is the equivalent of wanting desperately to get to the horizon that is spread out in every direction in front of us without realizing that we have been standing on it the entire time. We think that there is something better ahead of us and we get confused when, despite all of our trying, we can never seem to get there. All we have to do is stop looking at *beyond* where we are and start looking *at* where we are.

Me: There's nothing better ahead?

Myself: No.

Me: Well that's a depressing thought!

Myself: Are you depressed or did the thought make you depressed?

Me: What's the difference?

Myself: When you find your True self, you'll see.

Me: What will I see when I find my true self?

Myself: You will see that you are pure potential. How

could you become depressed without first having the potential to become depressed?

Me: I guess that makes sense.

Myself: The you that is "first," the you from which everything manifests is the you that you are searching for. At the core of your being you exist in a state of pure peace, silence, stillness, and harmony.

Me: Well that sounds nice, doesn't it? And you're telling me that I am in that state right now?

Myself: You are always in that state; you just have to realize it.

Me: How do I do that?

Myself: I'll show you later.

Me: Why don't you show me now?

Myself: I don't think you are yet ready to see **now**.

Me: Why not? How do you know?

Myself: It must be done in steps. Your concepts need to be stripped away one layer at a time.

When you learn to let go more and more of your internal thought processes, you will realize more and more of your True self. When you realize more of your True self, you will be operating from a higher degree of awareness and as a result you will experience a greater degree of freedom.

For example, if we draw a circle around a two dimensional stick figure that lives on a sheet of paper, we have placed a boundary around that person that limits their freedom. Now the stick figure can try to change the boundary conditions by somehow erasing the line, or by separating the line from the page in an attempt to go under the line, or it can leave the conditions as they are and transcend them. The stick figure can become a three dimensional person and simply step over the line that previously held it captive. It can do this because all of the information needed to replicate a multi-dimensional object can be stored onto an object with one less dimension (this is a scientific fact). The problem is that as long as the stick figure keeps trying to change the boundary conditions around it, it will never realize that it contains the power to transcend all boundaries and free itself.

A two dimensional stick figure holds the potential to become a three dimensional entity. A three dimensional entity holds the potential to become a four dimensional human. A four dimensional human holds the potential to become a five dimensional angel. Each time a person lets go of an old thought process, they make a quantum leap into a higher dimension and into a greater level of freedom. Eventually the boundaries themselves fade away and the ultimate (and original) state of unity is achieved.

True freedom comes when we are able to heal the separation within ourselves. When we finally do this we will laugh at ourselves for believing that a mark on a page could ever keep us imprisoned.

Me: And we heal this separation within ourselves by letting go of our internal thought processes?

Myself: Yes.

Me: You're basically saying that the things I believe, rather than *help* me in life, actually *make my life worse*?

Myself: Only if you believe that your beliefs are the Truth.

There exists two realities; the reality that we believe, and True Reality. **The reality that we believe, the reality *of* beliefs, is an illusion, and True Reality is the Reality *beyond* beliefs.** True Reality is beyond belief because you don't have to believe in It. You don't have to believe in It because It *is* It.

Me: This sure would be easier if you made any sense at all when you spoke.

Myself: Stay with me now. One has to believe that the illusion is real because it exists. One does not have to believe that Reality is real because *It is existence Itself.* One has to believe *that* something exists, but one does not have to believe *in existence.*

Let's say that you and I are driving down a back road in the country and off in the distance we spot an animal that is obviously some kind of a canine, but it is too far away to determine if it's a dog or a coyote. I may believe that it's a coyote and you may believe that it's a dog, but there is no need to believe that it *is*. The problem that we create for ourselves is that far too often we focus on what we *believe* instead of focusing on simply what *is*. Instead of enjoying the experience of sharing existence with another being, we argue and try to convince each other that my belief is right and your belief is wrong. The Truth of the matter is that all beliefs are right *and* wrong. They are right in that they describe Reality, and they are wrong in that that description will never be a perfect or complete description. A description is not what something actually is, a description is our attempt to share our experience of that something.

Me: Okay, but what if when we got close enough to that canine, we could both see that it was obviously a dog? Then that would make me right and you wrong. The more information that we can gather about something, the easier it is to determine who's belief is right and who's belief is wrong. You're basically saying that ignorance is bliss. The less you question things the easier it is to agree with other people, but if you never question anything how are you ever going to learn anything? People in comas don't get into very many disagreements but I sure wouldn't want to live like that. The dog was a dog regardless of what our individual beliefs were. It's up to you to admit that your belief was wrong and to see it for what it is.

Myself: I agree with you, but which definition of the dog is the ultimate definition? Is there a point where there will be absolutely no doubt as to what in fact we are attempting to describe?

Me: What do you mean? It's a dog. That's it. That is what it is. It's a dog. Got it?

Myself: Don't get snotty. I know it's a dog, but that's what it is only from a certain perspective. When we were more distant from the dog, the description became more general and the dog became a canine.

Me: The dog didn't become a canine, it always was a canine. We just became more specific when we got closer and could describe it precisely.

Myself: Okay, then let's keep getting closer and see if we can come up with an even more precise description of the canine, oh, I mean dog.

From 200 meters away we described it as a canine. From 20 meters away we described it as a dog. From 2 centimeters away we would describe it as fur because all we could see in our field of vision would be fur.

Now let's say that we used a microscope to look at it even closer. From hundredths of a millimeter away we would describe it as a cell because it would fill our entire field of vision. You would no longer be able to see the fur. If we were to increase the magnification further and look at it closer, we would describe it as a molecule; we would no longer be able to see the cell. Look at it from closer still and we would describe it as an atom; we would no longer be able to see the molecule. Closer yet and we would describe it as a subatomic particle. At this point there would be no way to tell what we were looking at because everything looks the same. We could describe what you were looking at as an electron, but there would be no way to tell *who's* electron it was because all electrons are exactly alike. If we were to look at it this close, "it" loses its meaning because "it" can no longer be distinguished from what it is that is looking at "it." In the realm of subatomic particles, the dog, the microscope, us, and everything else is made of the same stuff, which makes it impossible to tell where one thing ends and another thing begins. "It" at this point could be anything.

If we continue to look beyond the realm of subatomic particles at It (whatever *it* is at this point) we would eventually no longer be able to describe It with any certainty at all. At this point any attempt at description becomes futile because we are so close to it that we are no longer "away" from It at all. There is no "dog" and no "us", there is only "It".

It's important here to see that "It" never changed, only our perspective of It changed. It was always It, but we kept changing our description of It as our perspective of It changed. If we were both looking at It from 200 meters away, we could agree that It was some kind of a canine. As our perspective changed as we got closer, so did our description of It.

But what would have happened if I was looking at It through a particle accelerator and you were looking at It from 20 meters away? Surely you describing It as a dog would be no more right or wrong than my description of It as an electron. We of course were looking at the same thing and were simply calling It different names. The point is that at the end of our search for It, It turned out to be All the same thing. We are all looking at the same thing and just calling It different names. The only instance where one could possibly say that one of the descriptions was wrong was when I described It as a coyote instead of a dog. If I would have just left my description of It as a canine until I was sure what It was, we would never have been in disagreement at all. You had the better eyesight and therefore could provide a more accurate description of what It was. So the only time that someone was wrong (in disagreement with someone else) was when I guessed at what kind of a canine It was before I could see It clearly. Instead of guessing, I should have just said "I don't know what It is." In the end it turns out that that's what we should have done at the beginning.

Me: What do you mean?

Myself: There is a point where definitions are no longer possible. When we are 20 meters away from a canine, we can definitely call It a dog. When we are 10^{-33} centimeters away from It we can't definitely call It anything. The reason why we can't call It anything at this point is because at this magical distance (physicists call it the Planck length), the laws of physics break down. The laws of physics *are* how we describe how the universe exists. "Physics" is the study of physical "things." If physics can no longer describe It, It by definition is no longer a thing. It is no thing. What started out as "something" off in the distance, became "nothing" when there was no longer any distance.

Me: Wait a minute, how can there be no distance? If there is no distance left between us and what we are looking at, then there is no space, and since space and time are mutually dependant, then if there is no space, there is no time. Surely there must always be some distance between us and what we are looking at, even if it is such a small distance that we can no longer measure it.

Myself: I'm glad that you brought up time because at this point it may be easier to think in terms of time instead of space. Instead of trying to find out exactly *what* some*thing* is, let's try to find out exactly *when* some*time* is. Let's try to find out exactly when tomorrow is.

Basically what we are doing is exchanging the separation between two things, us and the dog, for the separation between two times, today and tomorrow. Just as there was a thing off in the distance that we called a dog, now there is a time off in distance that we call tomorrow. And just as we got as close as we could to find out exactly *what* the dog was, we are going to get as close to tomorrow as we can to see exactly *when* it is.

So now instead of two things being separated by meters and centimeters, we have two times separated by minutes and seconds. A clock that registers seconds is more accurate than a clock that only registers minutes. The clock that is able to split up time into the smallest bits is the most accurate and therefore the most able to tell us *exactly* when tomorrow comes. If you envision a stopwatch with a bunch of zeroes lined up to the left of the decimal point, then the stopwatch with the most zeroes (before we started them) would tell us best when tomorrow is. Not only that, but if we programmed two different stopwatches to automatically stop when they each reached midnight, the one with the most zeroes after the decimal point would stop *after* the one with less zeroes (which means that we would have to wait longer for tomorrow to arrive!?). Knowing that a stopwatch with the greater number of places after the decimal point (which denotes seconds) is the most accurate one, then a stopwatch with infinite places after the decimal point would be the most accurate one possible. The only problem with this is that a stopwatch that has infinite "'ths" of a second that is programmed to automatically stop when it reaches tomorrow will continue to run indefinitely. Such a clock will never get to tomorrow because it would be just too darn busy trying to calculate when exactly tomorrow is! "A watched pot never boils" or "tomorrow never comes," you pick the cliché.

Me: I follow your logic, but I can't help but get the feeling that you're just pulling a fast one on me somehow. How could tomorrow never get here just because we were looking really close for it?

Myself: Tomorrow never gets here when we look really close for it because there is no tomorrow to get here in the first place. Time is the measurement of the separation between events and space is the measurement of the separation between objects. An event is an action; it is when something happens. So if an event is when something happens, it needs something to do the happening. If we apply this to today and tomorrow, we see that in order to come up with the times "today" and "tomorrow" we have measured the event of the earth spinning as it orbits the sun. It is logical to choose the earth and the sun as the things to do the happening because they are the most common and reliable objects that we all experience. We have two things, now all we have to do is measure what they are doing.

When we measure what they are doing, it appears as though the sun comes up on one side of the earth and then goes down on the other side. One "day" is the measurement of the separation between when the sun appears at one side of the earth and the next time it appears at that same side. However, this measurement is valid only from our perspective here on the surface of the earth. If we were to leave the surface of the earth and observe the process from a perspective that allowed for a more complete description out in space, we would see that there is in fact no separation between what we call "today" and "tomorrow." What appeared as the sun coming up and going down when we were on the surface of the earth can now be seen as the earth spinning as it orbits around the sun. From our new vantage point we can see that what once was day and night, today and tomorrow, is merely the shifting of light to shadow as the sun shares its energy with the earth. Indeed from the perspective of the sun itself, night never even occurs on earth.

We can describe this using the concept of dimensions. When we were on the surface of the earth, we were experiencing a three dimensional process from a two dimensional perspective. From this limited view of the process it appeared as though the sun was coming up and going down. When we left the surface of the earth what we effectively did was transcend to a higher dimension, and from that higher dimension we could see that it wasn't so much as case of up and down as it was a case of around and around. Up and down are opposites, but around is the same thing. Up and down are two, around is one. Time is a description of a higher dimensional system that has been observed from a lower dimensional perspective.

When we transcend to higher levels of awareness, what were once seen as dualities such as right and wrong, dog and us, today and tomorrow, can be seen from a more complete perspective. Once seen from this higher perspective, these dualities do not so much disappear, but are no longer needed because a more complete and comprehensive understanding of Reality may now be utilized. A more complete and comprehensive understanding of Reality leads to less confusion and less confusion leads to the freedom to live Life instead of trying to figure It out.

It is interesting that scientists have discovered that the four seemingly separate forces that describe how the physical realm operates, become unified when looked at from the perspective of higher dimensions. Physicists have found that when they expand our physical realm that consists of four dimensions (length, width, depth, and time) to one that consists of ten dimensions, that all forces that appeared to be separate actually become one all encompassing and unified force. When we are able to see and experience Reality at a deeper and more comprehensive level, things that seemed to be different turn out to actually be the same.

Me: I'm confused about confusion. Earlier you said that it was good to be confused because that means that one was thinking beyond ones' usual parameters, and lately you've been saying that confusion inhibits ones freedom to live Life to its' fullest. Why the contradiction?

Myself: Thinking beyond our usual parameters is necessary *to a point.* A point is a zero dimensional entity. A zero dimensional entity is nothing because It cannot be defined. To define something is to "fix the bounds or limits of." Thinking beyond those limits leads us to a more comprehensive description of Reality, but ultimately Reality is *beyond thinking itself.* We don't say, "I can *know* your point" we say, "I can *see* your point." We can always think beyond boundaries to higher or deeper levels, but to be at a certain level, even the highest level, is to define that state and to therefore place boundaries upon It. If It has boundaries, then there must be something beyond It and if there is something beyond It, It cannot be the final state. **Thinking beyond** transcends us *to* a higher level, whereas **beyond thinking** transcends us *from* levels altogether.

We put up a boundary with our thoughts and then we overcome that boundary with another thought. But the very thought that allowed you to overcome the previous boundary has created its own boundary. This is the cycle of karma and the only way to break it is to stop trying to overcome boundaries and just stop putting them up in the first place. Thinking is the process of putting up boundaries and then overcoming them. Unfortunately, this cycle can never be resolved. Wisdom is not putting up boundaries in the first place.

Me: So I should just stop thinking?

Myself: You should stop thinking that the answer to your problems lies within your thoughts.

We are like the typical three-year old child that asks the same question over and over again. You know how that goes: "Where did that come from?" Answer. "Where did *that* come from?" Answer. "Where did *that* come from?" Answer: "I don't know!" or "It came from God!" Both answers are valid because ultimately we don't know, and "God" is the symbol that we use to describe the unknowable. Whether a person would like to admit it or not, the most brilliant scientist on earth can be stumped by a three-year old child. It isn't a matter of one being able to outwit the other; it's a matter of one being able to outlast the other. Is there ever an answer that allows no room for another question to be asked? Will there ever be an answer that renders all further questions unnecessary?

Any answer that we can come up with is restricted to the same limits that the question posed is. We are restricted to (by) the limits of thought, and thought is further restricted to (by) the limits of language. Questions are formed by the thinking mind and the resulting answer is formed by the same thinking mind.

Albert Einstein said, “One cannot solve a problem with the same mind that created the problem.” This of course means that we must look at the problem from a different perspective, but what if it is the thinking mind itself that is causing the problem? If we think up questions with our thinking mind and if we are to believe Mr. Einstein (a pretty safe bet), then we must come to the conclusion that we must go beyond the thinking mind to find Truth. The Truth that is spoken of in this regard is capitalized because It is Truth beyond what our thinking minds can possess. The truth that we seek by trying to know everything is attained by **thinking beyond**, but the Truth that needs no seeking is **beyond thinking**.

Me: Could you repeat that, I’m still confused.

Myself: You think you’re funny, don’t you?

Me: I’m only half joking. You tell me that we need to transcend to higher levels, but then you tell me that we have to get rid of levels altogether. You say that in order to find what we are looking for we have to stop looking for it. Confusion is good, but only to a point. Well, I’m tellin’ ya, I don’t think that I’m at that point yet.

Myself: Okay, let’s tackle this thing head-on. You want confusion; I’ll give you confusion.

“This statement is false.”

Think about this for a while. What we have here is the perfect paradox. If the statement true, then it is false. But if it is false, how can it be true?

Me: …I hate you.

Myself: You don’t hate *me*, you hate being confused. The reason why this statement causes our heads to spin is because it contains two levels of Truth and we are putting them on the same level. The primary level of Truth is the statement itself and the secondary level of truth is the description *of* the statement. The description of the statement tells us that the statement itself is false. The statement itself just is. Why does the description of the statement not coincide with the statement itself? There is nothing contained in the statement declaring that it is true, so why does describing it as false cause a problem for us?

Me: I don't know, but I don't like trying to figure it out. It hurts my brain.

Myself: The statement doesn’t have to declare itself as being true because the statement is Truth itself. The statement *is*. “Is” denotes existence. Existence is ultimate Truth. The universe does not lie. **Everything is exactly what it is; it is not something else. To be exact is to be perfect. Everything is perfect**. Imperfection arises in our attempt to define exactly what that thing is. The definition of something is not exactly what it is; it is something else. Statements like the one above throw us for a loop because we believe so strongly that the definition of something is actually what it is. This belief is a delusion. All beliefs, even ones that everyone around you accepts, are a type of delusion, and therefore lead to confusion. Once we realize that all attempts to define Reality are inherently incomplete, we need never be confused again because, knowing this, we believe them only *to a point*. Remember that a point has no dimensions. There are no limits or boundaries to a point and therefore one cannot define (place the limits or boundaries of) it.

Me: So definitions are pointless?

Myself: Insofar as they have no conclusion, yes. Definitions are the limits and boundaries that we place around the point. The only reason that we define things is so that we can share our experience of Reality with others, and we will never stop experiencing Reality. Communication is a tool for sharing, but far too often we use it to try to convince ourselves, and others, that our beliefs about Reality are the correct beliefs. That's why most of us surround ourselves with other people that have the same belief system that we do. If there are a lot of people around that think the same way you do, it's easier to convince yourself that Reality is actually what you think It is. If *our* version of Reality is the right one (and *we* all agree that it is) *theirs* must be wrong if *their* version is different than ours. Well, I hate to break it to ya, but if you have a version of Reality, it's wrong. Reality is Truth and any version of Reality is not Truth itself, but a version of Truth.

Me: So where does that leave us? If all of our versions of Reality are wrong, then communication is moot and so is this book.

Myself: It is kind of a catch-22 situation because we are using this book of concepts and ideas to lead us to a point beyond concepts and ideas. Books are one of the most valuable tools used to guide us on our journey of enlightenment, but they are only tools. This book is to be used as a map to help you learn the way to yourself, for yourself. Once you learn the way, you know it. Once you know the way, there is no longer any reason to consult the map. You know the way home from work; you don't have to carry around a map of the city with you just in case you get lost. If you have to constantly keep looking at a map to find your way home, either the map you have isn't very clearly written, or you're reading it wrong, or a combination of the two. A well-designed map should show you clearly and precisely the most efficient route that you should take to get to your destination. Once you have found that route, all that remains is to rehearse it to memory. Once you have rehearsed the route to memory, you will **know** it, and once you know it, it will come naturally, effortlessly to you. This rehearsing of the route to memory is what we could call "Spiritual practice."

Me: I knew that you where going to get religious on me eventually.

Myself: Who said anything about religion?

Me: Well isn't Spiritual practice religion?

Myself: Spiritual practice is the way in which we realize our true selves. Our true selves - what we really are - is Spirit, and we practice being ourselves until we are being ourselves at all times and in all places. Religion is a form of Spiritual practice, but I wouldn't say that Spiritual practice is exclusively designated to religion. The various religions practiced throughout the world are all designed to focus our attention on Spirit. However one cannot, and must not, restrict Spirit by designating It to religion exclusively. **If we are Spiritual beings, then there cannot be a time or a place where we are not being Spiritual**. I am at all times and at all places, me. I am me at church. I am me washing the dishes. I am me at work. I am me playing golf. Every experience that I am a part of is an expression of Spirit and deserves, requires, my full and undivided attention. In this way, every experience, (the) All experience, is a religious experience, and All of life is sacred.

Me: You said that what we really are is Spirit. Could you elaborate on that?

Myself: There are three aspects used to describe what a human is. These aspects are mind, body, and Spirit. This triune system is a representation of Reality Itself. This is the process of All. It is You, It is Me, It is the Rock, It is the Galaxy, It is the Atom, It is God, It is One, Every, and None. It is All. When people ask: "what is it?" this is what "it" is. This is IT:

-	0	+
NEGATIVE	NEUTRAL	POSITIVE
MIND	SPIRIT	BODY
PAST	PRESENT	FUTURE
BIRTH	LIFE	DEATH
HOLY GHOST	FATHER	SON
SUBJECT	REALITY	OBJECT
YIN	TAO	YANG
WAVE	ENERGY	PARTICLE
THOUGHT	POTENTIAL	ACTION

Each triune is a representation of a system. -, 0, +, is a representation of the numerical system. Mind, Spirit, body, is a representation of the human system. It's probably best to start with the human system because it's the one that we are most familiar with.

When people are asked to name the different aspects of a human being, the definitions of mind, body, and Spirit are given. It is a universal description that is accepted by all people from all cultures. In order to know what Spirit is, we also need to know what mind and body are because Spirit is the harmony of mind and body.

We don't have much of a problem relating to the body aspect of being human, but mind and Spirit are a little more difficult to get a handle on. Mind and body are aspects of Spirit like heads and tails are aspects of a coin.

The philosopher Rene Descartes gave perhaps the most compelling proof of existence with the famous quote: "I think, therefore I am." It's hard to argue with that one. In this statement, he is saying that mind is proof of matter. If we turn the statement around to read "I am, therefore I think," we would be saying that matter is also proof of mind.

Me: Are you suggesting that everything has a mind?

Myself: Not so much that everything *has* a mind, as everything *is* mind. Let me put it to you this way: Let us say that you (your Spirit) reside in your body. While you are alive, awake, and conscious, you are always there. This would mean that you (your Spirit) are always in the same place (your body) at different times. You were in your body at 9:15 p.m. on December 22, 2001, and you were in your body at 6:12 p.m. yesterday evening. To bring this concept a little closer to home, we could say that you (your body) were home (in your house) at 9:15 p.m. on December 22, 2001, and you were home yesterday at 6:12 p.m. The point is that you can be in the same place at different times. This is how you exist in the realm of matter.

You exist in the *same place at different times* as your body and you exist in the *same time at different places* as your mind. What exists at the same time at different places?

Me: Everything!

Myself: A part of you is your body and a part of you is the entire universe! If we were to compare this description of a human to the numerical system, my body would be #32,560,143,628,554,810,006,374 and your body would be #32,560,143,628,554,814,427,169, but our mind would be the entire number system itself. We are of the same mind, and yet we are of different bodies.

Quantum physics…

Me: Oh no. This is going to be complicated, isn't it?

Myself: …AHEM! Quantum physics is a branch of science that tries to find out what physical reality is made of by breaking It down into the smallest bits that it can. It's basically the same idea that we had when we looked at that dog to see what it really was. Quantum physics has discovered that when we break "things" (from rocks, to dogs, to humans) down to the smallest bits that we can, "things" become harder and harder to define. If you remember, when we looked at the dog so closely that we found an electron, we couldn't be sure whose electron it was because all electrons are exactly alike. What physicists did is that they shot a single electron through an opening in a barrier and recorded where it landed on the other side. Then they placed another opening in the barrier next to the first opening and shot another single electron at the barrier. The result was one of the most astonishing revelations about how Reality works to ever be discovered.

What they discovered was that subatomic particles such as electrons and photons are not only particles like baseballs, but are also waves, like the waves created on the surface of a lake when you throw a baseball into it. The experiment that proves this fact goes like this:

When physicists shot a single electron through an opening in a barrier a number of times and recorded where the electron hit the target placed on the other side, they found that there was an area behind the opening where the electron was most likely to hit. This of course comes as no surprise. The scattering of holes in the target would very much resemble a shotgun blast with most of the holes near the centre, and progressively fewer holes as we moved away from the centre. The surprise came when they added a second opening in the barrier right next to the first one. When a single electron was randomly shot at both openings a number of times, the result was not the same shotgun blast-like pattern, but a pattern that had areas within the shot gun blast-like pattern where the electron would not travel. The addition of a second opening next to the original opening affected how the electron would go through the original opening.

When you first hear of this experiment it's easy to miss the full ramifications of what this finding really means. In the first part of the experiment, an electron traveling though the opening struck the target and created a pattern that looked like a shotgun blast. In the second part of the experiment, an electron traveling through the same opening when there was a neighbouring opening did not strike the target in the same manner. The pattern created in the second part of the experiment looked like a shotgun blast with lines running through it, indicating areas where the electron did not strike the target. Why would the addition of a second opening affect the way in which an electron went through the original opening? Somehow the electron "knew" that there was a second opening in the barrier and it changed its behaviour accordingly.

This "knowing" is the wave aspect of a particle. When the electron went through the openings, it did so not only like a baseball, but also like a wave.

If we were to place a barrier in a tank of water and repeat the same experiment as the one described above, we could quite accurately reproduce the wave aspect of a particle. This time instead of shooting the particle through the openings, we will drop the particle into the water and observe how the water travels through them.

When we drop the particle into the water, it creates a disturbance on the surface of the water that travels outward in all directions. We've known this fact ever since we could throw a rock into a puddle. When the wave meets a barrier with an opening in it that is narrower than the distance between crests of the wave itself, it will go through the opening and spread out in all directions behind the opening as it continues traveling. If we were to relate this concept to the particle part of this experiment, it would be much like how shotgun pellets spread out after leaving the muzzle of the barrel. When the wave meets a barrier with an opening in it that is wider than the distance between the crests of the wave itself, it will not spread out behind the opening as it continues traveling. This would be like a how a rifle bullet travels in the same straight line after it leaves the muzzle of the rifle.

When a wave meets a barrier with two openings in it that are narrower than the distance between the crests of the wave, it will in effect break into two separate waves at each opening and spread out as they continue traveling. When the two waves meet, they interfere with each other, which causes some crests to rise higher and some crests to disappear. If you've ever seen the wakes of two boats meeting, you kind of get the idea (especially if you happened to be water-skiing behind one of them). Where the crest of one wave meets the crest of the other wave, the two join forces and create a much larger and more powerful single wave. Where the crest of one wave meets the trough of the other wave, they cancel each other out and the water is still.

This interaction and convergence of the two waves is what creates the patterns that appear on the target placed behind the openings in the barrier. The places where the crest of one wave meets the crest of the other wave is where the electron hit the target more often. The places where the crest of one wave meets the trough of the other wave is where the electron hit the target less often.

The mathematical representation of this wave-like quality that particles possess is called the "wave function." The wave function of a particle is the mathematical expression of all the various possible states of that particle. The wave function is an expression of what is possible. A *part*icle is that possibility defined (to fix the bounds or limits of).

Michio Kaku, in his book *Hyperspace*, wrote the following description of the wave function: "If I could somehow see my own wave function, it would resemble a cloud very much in the shape of my body. However, some of the cloud would spread out over all space, out to Mars and even beyond the solar system, although it would be vanishingly small there." Our bodies are one possible state of our mind, which is all possible states. Our existence is not limited to our bodies. Each of our bodies is only one outcome out of all possible outcomes. Mind is possibility; body is possibility defined, limited.

Me: So what you're saying is that the wave function is actually a description of our mind?

Myself: Yes.

Me: Wow! If that's true, it's huge!

Myself: Quantum physics has looked at the smallest chucks of matter and have found that at the very foundation of physical reality is a place (or possibly more like a state) where the laws of physics break down. This state is mind. Concepts such as "force", "cause", "know", and "free will" are all describing this state.

Me: Didn't you say earlier that the universe was our mind?

Myself: When I say "the universe," I'm speaking of the wave function in its' manifest state at a specific point in time. We can't conceptualize mind in its' inherent state because it is by definition a non-thing. Your wave function is every possible outcome existing at once. The easiest way of looking at it is that your mind is everything and your body is one thing of that everything. When I say "the universe," I am talking about this "everything."

Me: Okay, back to Spirit then. Spirit is…

Myself: Spirit is the unity of body and mind. **The harmony of your body and your universe is Spirit.** We exist in the same place at different times in the form of our bodies. We exist in the same time at different places in the form of our mind. We *are existence* in the same time and place as Spirit.

Spirit is the relationship between the body-mind; between the one and the every. The one is not other than the every and the every is not other than the one, much like how an individual is not other than society and society is not other than the individual.

We must stop associating who we are as simply our physical bodies. You do not stop at your skin. Your body is only one frame of reference for your mind.

Me: What do you mean by the statement: "your body is only one frame of reference for your mind?"

Myself: Your mind is all possible states of existence. That means that everything from the subatomic particle to the entire universe is you. Your body just happens to be the form that you have chosen to define as yourself.

Where do you end and the rest of the Universe begin?

Me: That seems pretty obvious doesn't it?

Myself: It seems pretty obvious if I ask it while standing six feet away from you, but what if I asked it from a different perspective? If we go back to the experiment where we looked at the dog and put you in place of the dog, we will find that once again each perspective requires a different answer. When we're six feet away, it appears as though you end and the Universe begins at the edge of your skin. When we get so close to you that all we see is your cells, it appears as though you end and the rest of the universe begins at the edge of your cell. When we get so close to you that all we can see is your molecules, it appears as though you end and the Universe begins at the edge of your molecule. When we look so close to you that all we can see is your atoms, it appears as though you end and the universe begins at the edge of your atom.

What if we were to pull our perspective back now? Which perspective is the correct one on which to base your identity? When we looked at your atom, the universe appeared to be outside of the atom. However, the atom is a part of your body, so the space that we see outside of the atom is actually you. When we see only the molecules again, the space outside of the molecules appears to be where the universe begins, when actually it is still a part of you. When we get to your cells, the space outside of your cells is still you. When we see your body, it appears as though you end and the universe begins at the edge of your skin, however, **the space outside of your skin is still you.** When we continue to pull our perspective back even farther, it appears as though you end and the rest of the universe begins at the edge of your earth. Back farther yet and you end and the universe begins at the edge of your solar system. One more level back and you end and the universe begins at the edge of your Milky Way galaxy.

We can keep going until we reach the edge of your universe.

Who and what "you" are is relative to the perspective taken. We assume that each of us is who and what we happen to see the most.

Who and what we are is Spirit. Spirit is the definition that we use to describe what we cannot describe. What phrase comes out most often at the moment of orgasm?

Me: Excuse me?

Myself: That's what you say when you have an orgasm: "excuse me."?

Me: No you big dummy, I'm expressing my shock at you asking such a question.

Myself: Oh come on, lighten up a little. What do you most often say when you have an orgasm?

Me: "Oh my God!"

Myself: What do you say when someone startles you?

Me: "Ahhhh!"

Myself: Okay. How about when you are in excruciating pain?

Me: "Oh my God this hurts!"

Myself: What do you say when you ache with sadness?

Me: "Oh God."

Myself: How about when you're really excited?

Me: "Oh my God!"

Myself: We use the word "God" to describe an experience that is beyond description. This is also true for "Spirit." It is impossible for us to intellectually understand and describe how something can be both a particle and a wave at the same time, or that you can be your body and the whole universe at the same time. Not that sometimes it's a particle and sometimes it's a wave, it is both simultaneously. Particle is not separate from wave and wave is not separate from particle. You are not separate from the universe and the universe is not separate from you. This is the same system that Christians speak of when they talk of the Holy Trinity. Christ is the body aspect of God just as a particle is the physical aspect of energy. Holy Ghost is the mind aspect of God just as wave is the non-physical aspect of energy. There is no God separate from the two aspects of It. It is unfortunate that we continue to take so literally the father-son analogy given in Christ's time to describe this relationship of mind and body, thought and action.

Me: Are you saying that there is no God?

Myself: **I'm saying that there is nothing *but* God.**

God is the process.

Me: The process of what?

Myself: It.

Me: What is "It"?

Myself: The process.

Me: The process of what?

Myself: God.

Me: Why do I feel like I just stepped into an Abbott and Costello routine?

Myself: God is **THE** process. The process of sameness and change, the process of birth and death, the process of body and mind. All of these seemingly opposing states are actually a single process that we have separated in an attempt to understand who we are.

There is an underlying symmetry and oneness to All. One could say that if there is a single law that governs the ongoing flow of existence, it is: "**THERE SHALL BE SYMMETRY!**" Physicists have found in their search for the primary particle of matter, what everything is made of, that everything is not made of a particle-ular "thing," but rather that "things" are only one aspect of a process. This process, and every sub-process, and every sub-sub process, is balanced, symmetrical, perfect. If one were to measure all of the crests against all the troughs of any wave, the end result would be stillness.

This is important. If we were sitting in a canoe on a perfectly still lake and someone dropped a boulder into the water just a few meters away, the waves created on the surface of the water would, of course, rock our little boat quite violently. The stillness of the lake represents pure potential, pure energy, nothing. When the boulder is dropped into the water, it creates a disturbance in the field of energy in the form of the waves upon which we are bobbing up and down. While there may be periods where the canoe is tilting, going up, going down, spinning around, if we were to measure all of the action that took place, the net result would be zero. *Nothing* happened, or, nothing *happened.* Either way of looking at it is valid.

All is perfectly balanced. For every crest of a wave there is a trough. For every particle that spins in one direction, there is a particle that spins in the opposite direction. For every particle there is an antiparticle. This is the system, the process. There is energy, which is defined as: "the potential for action," and there is the manifestation of that potential into (as) two equal and mutually dependent halves.

Me: In that last paragraph you used the words "opposite" and "anti", and then you go on to say that these opposing halves are mutually dependant. Which is it? Are they fighting against each other or are they working together with each other?

Myself: Both.

Me: Somehow I knew that you were going to say that.

Myself: It all depends upon your interpretation of the system. When a particle meets up with its antiparticle, both entities are mutually annihilated and only pure energy, or if you like, nothing, remains. This conversion of matter to energy is the most efficient known to man. The conversion of matter to energy that takes place in the fusion explosion of a hydrogen bomb is about 1% efficient. In comparison, the conversion of matter to energy that takes place in a matter-antimatter interaction is 100% efficient.

There are two ways in which to interpret such an interaction. One way is to see the mutual annihilation of the two particles as death, as a ceasing of existence, and as such we could easily depict such an occurrence as a battle for survival in which there is no winner. We could also see it as the reunification of the two aspects of energy back into pure potential. In the first description of the event, we have interpreted the interaction between a particle and its antiparticle as a battle. In the second description of the event, we have interpreted the same interaction as mutual cooperation.

Me: Which interpretation is the right one?

Myself: Once again it's not so much a case of which one is right and which one is wrong, as it is a case of which one provides a more complete description of the process. When we described the spinning of the earth as it orbits around the sun as the sun coming up and going down, we were assigning a single process dualistic properties. We did this because we were viewing a three dimensional process from a two dimensional perspective. We could not see the process as a whole so we misinterpreted what was actually happening.

When we don't see the whole process - All - it is easy to misinterpret It as a bunch of separate and opposing parts. When we see the sun going down, it is easy to forget that viewed from the other side of the earth, it is coming up. Going down is coming up and coming up is going down. Death is birth, birth is death. There are no opposing forces. Death is not the opposite of Life. *Birth and death are the two aspects of Life.* Life does not just go away. The sun does not just go away when we can't see it anymore. Energy shifts and changes. Life shifts and changes. **Death is not non-Life, *death is life changing*.**

Me: Death is Life changing. I like that. That's what people who have had a near-death experience say. So there is life after death?

Myself: The process of Life is birth and death. We think that death is non-Life, but there is no such thing as non-Life. Life is all there is. There is no such thing as "non." To "not to be" is to change. It is possible to be and it is possible to change. It is impossible not to be. It is possible to be who you are and it is possible to change. It is not possible to not be who you are.

Me: "To be or not to be, that is the question."

Myself: To be *and* not to be, that is the answer. "To be"

is to remain the same, and "not to be" is to change. When we ask the question "why," the answer is "because." To "be" is to remain the same, and to "cause" is to change.

Let's say that you are lying on the couch. There are essentially two options that you have to choose from. You may remain lying on the couch and you may get off of the couch and do something else. At the most basic level of *description* of Reality, there are two choices to be made. One is the choice to remain the same and the other is the choice to change. This is where it gets a bit tricky.

The choice to remain the same must always be, because if it changed, it would not be what it is - the choice to remain the same. Time is not a factor in this equation. "1" does not cease to exist when we move onto "2". It is not so much a case of you *were* doing something and *then* you *were* doing something else, as it is a case of you *are* doing something *and* you *are* doing something else.

Me: How can I remain lying on the couch and get up off of the couch and do something else at the same time?

Myself: In the form of your mind. Remember that your mind is all possibilities and your body is the manifestation of one of those possibilities. This holds true for all events just as it does for all "things."

Brian Greene stated the following in his book *The Fabric Of The Cosmos* the following: "In this way of thinking, events, regardless of when they happen from any particular perspective, just *are*. They all exist. They eternally occupy their particular point in spacetime. If you were having a great time at the stroke of midnight on New Year's Eve, 1999, you still are, since that is just one immutable location in spacetime. It is tough to accept this description, since our worldview so forcefully distinguishes between past, present, and future. But if we stare intently at this familiar temporal scheme and confront it with the cold hard facts of modern physics, its only place of refuge seems to lie within the human mind." Time and individual events lie within the human mind, but the universal mind is everything at once. Everything we have done and everything we will do is all "still" there and "already" there. It is essentially timeless. In our universal mind, nothing "flows" or "passes." It all just is.

Me: That quote blows my mind; my *human* mind, that is. And this guy knows what he's talking about.

Myself: It does, doesn't it. It really brings into question all of our concepts of free will and our experience of time. And yes, this guy definitely knows what he is talking about!

Me: So my mind is everything that I have done and everything that I will do.

Myself: When we are talking in terms actions; of time, yes. When we are talking in terms of objects; of space, it is every physical thing.

Me: And what's the difference between my human mind and my universal mind?

Myself: Your human mind is every event that you have experienced, and will experience from the perspective of your present human body. Your human mind is every event in your Life that you record with your human brain from the moment you were born until the moment that you die.

Your universal mind is every event that you have experienced from the perspective of the entire universe. Your universal mind is every event in your Life that you record with your evolving brain from the moment you were born *at the big bang* until the moment the universe dies.

Me: It sounds like I'm living a double life.

Myself: When we describe our Life, it sounds like we are living a double Life.

We are trying to describe how we exist in the cycle of existence. From a certain perspective we exist *in* the cycle of existence. From this perspective we are living a double Life. From a certain (non) perspective, we *are* the cycle of existence. From *this* (non) perspective, we are Living a single Life; or if you wish, *we are Life itself.*

My body was born and my body will die. The **I** that is experiencing Reality with my body is Life itself. The universe was born and will die. The **WE** that is experiencing Reality with (as) the universe is Life itself. Birth and death is the cycle of Life.

Me: So the part of me that is my body was born in 1969 and the part of me that is the universe was born at the big bang. The whole of me, the cycle itself, is Life.

Myself: That's right. The universe that we can see came into being about 14 billion years ago in an event that we have entitled the "Big Bang." The title of "Big Bang" is a little bit deceiving because the universe started out so small that It was impossible to measure. Actually, calling It "small" is rather a moot point if you can't measure It because if you can't measure It how can you assign a size to It? At any rate, the universe at this point is a point. It is a zero dimensional entity of pure potential.

This "zero dimensional entity of pure potential" has been called a "singularity" by physicists because in It All forces and All matter are unified into a single whatever-the-heck-It-is. This is why It is immeasurable. It is immeasurable not so much because It is so "small" that It can't be measured, It is immeasurable because there is nothing else to measure It against. Something is "small" only when it is compared to something that is "big." Something is "big" only when compared to something that is "small." In a singularity there are no separate entities. There is no one thing that is "big" and another thing that is "small", there is only one thing, and It just *is*.

We all came from, are, and are going to, a single entity, a single consciousness that was fully aware of the reason why It was. It knew that the reason why It was is because. Why It is, is to be and to cause to be. Be-cause-be-cause-be-cause. Why It is, is to remain the same and to change. It is free. It is free to be and not to be (change). It is free to know and not to know. It is the process of freedom Itself, and being so It chose to become, It chose to *be* and It chose to *come* into being. It became Adam; It became Atom; It became the first. And so "0" became "1", the hydrogen atom, the first element on the periodic table. And so "1" became "2", the helium atom, the second element on the periodic table. Each entity is the same consciousness that has made different choices. "0" is the choice to remain, and "1" is "0" that has made the choice to change. "2" is the choice that "1" has made to change and "1" is the choice that "1" has made to remain. "1" changes (dies) and becomes "2", but we have known ever since we were three years old when we learned to count that 1 does not cease to exist just *be-cause* it has moved onto "2". "1" has, is, and will always *be*, we have just shifted our focus, and that shifting of focus *causes* "2" to be.

Me: So what you are describing here is the act of creation.

Myself: Yes.

Me: You started off that last line of thought stating that choice was the driving force of creation, and then at the end you said that shifting of focus was the cause of being. Which is it? No, no, let me guess, it's both.

Myself: Well sort of, but I would say that "shifting of focus" is a more accurate description. "Choice" is the word that we use when we attempt to understand the “why” of our actions.

Let’s say that you go to the ice cream parlor to buy an ice cream cone. There are 27 different flavors to choose from and they come in three different sizes and two different varieties of cones. You walk out of the store with a medium sized “cookies and cream” waffle cone. Why?

Me: Because I chose to buy a medium sized “cookies and cream” waffle cone.

Myself: You are correct. Well at least half correct.

Me: I only half chose to by a medium sized “cookies and cream” waffle cone?

Myself: Well, as with every concept, there are two different ways in which to conceptualize the concept of choice. The one that you chose (or not chose), above is the concept of “free will”. “Free will” is of course the idea that we have control over our actions and that control allows us to decide our own fate via the choices that we make. The other way to conceptualize the system of choice is called “determinism”. “Determinism” is the idea that everything we do has been pre-determined and that we have no control over our actions. “Free will” is the concept of all choice and “determinism” is the concept of no choice, or if you will, control and no control. "Free will" is one extreme of the system of choice, and "determinism" is the other extreme of the system of choice.

“Choice” is the system of free will *and*

determinism. Depending on where your focus, or perspective is, one concept will seem to more completely describe your Reality.

Me: Okay... So how can I have different perspectives when I'm here in this body? Are there other perspectives from which I can experience Reality?

Myself: Your body is one aspect of a system. When you believe that you are only your body and that your mind is something separate, you are limiting your perspective to (by) that particular (*partical*-uar?) belief system.
Me: Okay... So that didn't clear it up for me.

Myself: Let me put it to you this way. Reality is analogous to a book. A book exists as a process where three seemingly separate parts work in harmony to create the whole. How much control we have over our lives depends upon which part we see ourselves playing in the process.

If we see ourselves as a character in the book (body), it seems as though we are merely playing out the role that the author of the book has written for us. If we see ourselves as author of the book (mind), it seems as though we have total control over what happens in the book. If we see ourselves as reader of the book (Spirit), the concept of control has become a moot point because we are the observer in the process. "Control" is merely a result of trying to define our actions in relation to the part of the process we choose to identify with. So the real choice is not so much what to do at any given moment as it is from which perspective of the process do you choose to experience Reality from?

It is as if we are acting in, writing, and reading our autobiography all at the same time.

Me: If we are acting in, writing, and reading all at the same time, where does that leave the concept of time itself? It seems so obvious to me that things happen in order, that there are things that cause other things to happen and that there is a definite progression through time. If mind is everywhere at once, shouldn't we be able to know the future as well as the past? The way you speak, it's almost as if the process itself has a timeless quality to it.

Myself: Excellent! That is a very astute observation.

Me: Oh stop, I'm blushing. So... do you have an answer, or are you trying to side-step the issue with unabashed flattery?

Myself: I don't have an answer, but I do have a very workable analogy (which is what an answer really is anyway; just a very good analogy). If we go back to looking at Reality as a book, we can understand the concept of causality, and as a result the concept of time, a little better.

The seemingly linear flow of time comes from the way we have agreed upon about how we will experience Reality. In the same way that we have agreed that we will read English from left to right and from the top down, we have agreed to experience Reality in the way we do. Everything is all just "there," as it is in a book. When we read it, we read it in a linear fashion. If we try to read the book in another way, like down - up, or right - left, it won't make any sense.

Me: And what about the not being able to see into the future thing?

Myself: If we are to assume our identity strictly from the perspective of the author, we are still bound from knowing the future because we can only know as much as we have written. This is why we can see only into the past. As long as the author is still unaware that he is in fact writing an autobiography, there will still exist the boundary of his thoughts, for one cannot think, by definition, beyond his thoughts. There will still be the question for the author of: "what lies beyond my thoughts?" or "where do my thoughts come from?" He is still separate from the character in the book, which is actually him that is acting out what he is writing, and therefore the system is not self contained and self fulfilled. In such a system there is mind, which tells the body what to do; thought comes first, then action. As a result, there is the appearance of a cause-effect, before-after timeline that starts as far "back" as his mind will allow (the beginning of the book), and ends at the point to which the book has been written. A person can look "back" on what he "has" written, but he cannot look "forward" to what he "will" write. Now for the "timeless" idea.

Albert Einstein once said: "people like us, who believe in physics, know that the distinction between past, present, and future is only a stubbornly persistent illusion." Perhaps we are at a point now to see how time is merely a stubbornly persistent illusion. If the author of the book were to simply realize that he is writing an autobiography, that is, that he is not separate from what he is writing, causality, and therefore, time, will be revealed as an illusion.

If the author of the book is writing her autobiography, then the source of her creativeness is the life that she has lived thus far, which is the very book that she is writing. From this perspective, the action of the character precedes the thought of the creator. However, if the character in the book is acting out the script that the author has written for her, then her actions are preceded by the thoughts of the creator. So which is the cause and which is the effect? The source of the characters' life comes from the script written by the author, but the source of the script written by the author comes from the characters life.

Me: Which came first, the chicken or the egg?

Myself: Precisely. That question is as redundant as asking: "which came first, the seed or the plant?" It is obvious that the seed contains within it the potential to grow the plant and the plant contains within it the potential to grow the seed. The seed grows the plant, the plant grows the seed. The creator creates the created, the created creates the creator. One is never separate from the other.

In an enlightened being, this process happens with no intermediate steps. The cycle happens instantaneously and spontaneously so that there is nothing to separate the person and what the person is doing.

Time is a measurement of the separation between events. We record events with our brain. When we remember an event, or create a fictional event through fantasy, we are in fact creating time. We have separated the All experience into two separate experiences. There is *that* event “back there,” or "in the future," and there is *this* event “here,” in the present.

Zen masters speak of a timeless experience where “this” and “that” merge into one. This is accomplished by attaining a state where no individual thoughts enter the mind. All experience is one complete and whole event. “This” and “that” have merged into “this,” into the present.

We have all had this experience of “losing our self” in our work or in a sport or in a book. We’ve got it a bit backwards. We don’t “lose ourselves” in this state, we actually *find* our selves in this state. We may lose our *sense* of self; the ego, but that is not our True self.

Athletes call this state “being in the Zone.” It is a state where all actions come absolutely effortlessly with no thought as to what should be done or how to do it. The opposite of this state as it relates to athletics is the act of “choking.”

Me: Ya, I know what that’s about. That’s when even the simplest things become very hard to do. I start to sweat and shake and question just about everything that I do. It usually happens when I’m under a lot of pressure.

Myself: What kind of pressure?

Me: Well, if there are a lot of people watching me, or if it's a real important game, or if there's money involved.

Myself: It's important to see that all of this pressure that you feel comes from your own subjective view of the situation. The rules of the game are exactly the same as they are when you are "in the Zone," so why can't you perform the same way?

Me: Because **there's too much pressure!**

Myself: There's only pressure because you *think* that there is. Your thoughts about all the people watching, and the money involved, and how important it is all interfere with the completion of the act itself.

If you think that there is a reason to do something other than the very act of doing the thing, it all falls apart. When people are in the Zone, they aren't thinking about anything other than what they are presently doing. They are completely present. The original goal of winning the game or the championship has taken a back seat to the immediate goal of simply playing the game to your best ability. All of these goals that we set for ourselves are really just answers we try to come up with for why we strive to be the best that we can. The real reason we do the best that we can is not to win or to make money. Those things may appeal to the ego, but when we act from Spirit, we find that every action is in and of itself the very goal that we are striving for.

Me: So the reason to do things is just to do them?

Myself: That's right. Every action carries with it its' own reward. When each and every action that one performs is done with perfect attention, each and every action is in and of itself completely fulfilling.

When your entire Life is in the Zone, each and every action in your Life will be completely fulfilling. Can you imagine how cool *that* would be? If everything that you did in your Life came absolutely effortlessly, and the result of everything that you did in your Life was the "best." If playing the best round of golf in your Life while in the Zone was a great experience, just think what a great experience your whole Life would be if you *lived* in the Zone!

Me: Is this where the role of the observer, or the reader of the book comes into this? The way to get into the Zone is by taking on the perspective of observer?

Myself: One does not really cause the other. When one is in the Zone, mind and body are working in harmony. When this happens, one is experiencing Life from a Spiritual level. One no longer has to really "try" to do anything, one simply does it. With no thoughts about what to do or how to do it, one is free to put all of ones' energy into the experience of the action. This is the direct experience of Reality. This is what the whole process is about. This "direct experience of Reality" is the reason for All existence.

Me: All of this is here simply to experience? All of

creation; all of this birth and death, all of the pain and joy, all of the questions and answers; all of it is being constructed for the simple reason of being experienced?

Myself: How could it be otherwise? Are we here simply to get to there? If that's the case, then being here can't be the reason for why we are here. If being here isn't the reason for being here, then there is no reason at all for being here because we are never anywhere else *but* here. Where are you right now?

Me: I'm here.

Myself: How about now?

Me: Still here.

Myself: What is the reason for writing a book?

Me: To share information, or to entertain.

Myself: And who is the receiver of the information? Who is the person being entertained?

Me: The reader.

Myself: Reality is the ultimate interactive experience. We are at once the players, authors, and readers of the most exquisite story ever written. When we fail to give It our full attention, we are doing a great disservice to ourselves, for there is nothing greater than, in fact there is nothing *other* than, It.

The character of the book acts out the book. The author of the book creates the book. The reader of the book gives it Life. A book sitting on a shelf may contain an entire world within its pages, but it is not until someone opens it up and begins reading it that that world comes to life. Quantum physicists actually have a version of this "unread book" state of the universe. They call this state the "virtual" state of the universe. Every event that will occur in the universe is contained in this virtual form until (a) consciousness brings it to Life. Quantum physics states that in order for something to exist, it must be observed.

Me: “If a tree falls in the forest and nobody is there to hear it, does it make any sound?”

Myself: “If a tree falls in the forest and nobody is there to hear it, what would be the point?”

Science has determined that the recording of an action is one of the steps required in order for something to exist. The act of observation is required in order for something to exist. The *quality of the observation* is the vehicle through which the quality of the object and act are revealed. We mistakenly believe that once we see something, we have seen it. That’s not completely true. There are different levels of seeing, understanding, and experiencing things.

We need to give Reality our full attention. We need to read the book!

The entire universe was created to be experienced by you. Your highest calling is to experience It to its fullest. We are created, we create, and we experience.

As we progress through the cycle of awareness, our Life-goal perspective will parallel this cycle.

We start off as mere creations with the main goal in Life being to survive. From this perspective it seems as though we have very little control over our Life. As our awareness of our true self grows, we become the creators of our own destiny. This perspective brings with it more control and the Life goal changes to the pursuit of knowledge and wisdom rather than material possessions. The ultimate perspective is that of the observer. This perspective includes all other perspectives simultaneously and therefore Life's goal becomes not just to survive or to create, but to do these things and to also have the full awareness of doing so.

The shifting of one's focus from the mere doing of the thing to having the full experience of the doing of the thing is very subtle, but it is also deeply profound.

Me: So you're implying that our focus should be more on *how* we are doing things rather than on what things we should be doing?

Myself: That is a very good way of putting it.

Me: I'm having a hard time with the idea of just letting go of trying to create our own destiny. You make it sound as if the whole idea of free will is just an illusion; that it doesn't really matter whether or not I have any likes and dislikes at all. It certainly *feels* as though I have preferences and that the actions of my Life come about out of my choosing one thing over another. Do we actually have no control over the things that we do?

Do we not have free will?

Myself: We do and we do not. There is no ultimate answer to that question. There is no answer to that question because, and this is the hard part to understand, all three perspectives exist simultaneously. We are at once acting in, writing, and reading the book. It is for this reason that any question regarding free will, any question *at all* for that matter, cannot be concluded with a "yes" or a "no" answer. The best answer I can give you is that we have no choice but to have infinite choices.

The statement "infinite choices" seems to be the ultimate expression of freedom, however, if we truly do have an infinite amount of different possibilities that we must choose from, then we are imprisoned just as surely as if we have no choice at all. If there is only one "right" or "best" thing to do in any given situation, and there are an infinite number of things to do at any given situation, then all of our energy must be put into the assessment of "which thing should I do?" Just like the stopwatch that put all of its' energy into calculating when tomorrow was going to arrive, if we are to believe that we are free to make any choice that we want, then we must put all of our energy into the calculation of what choice we should make.

True freedom is not really having the choice to do what we want, true freedom comes from being free from choices altogether. This doesn't mean that it is better to have no free will than to have total free will, it means that it is better to be free from the entire concept of choice itself.

There is really no "best" thing to do at the "top" of the list of things to do and there is no "worst" thing to do at the "bottom" of the list of things to do because there really is no list at all.

When we break Reality into separate, self contained entities like we do when we introduce the concept of individual choices, we create the illusion of discontinuity; the appearance of things stopping and starting. If things have beginnings and endings, then we can have conclusions like “this” and “that,” and “yes” and “no.” However, the findings of quantum physics have revealed that Reality does not consist of separate, self contained entities, but is a relationship, and that this relationship is ultimately indescribable.

It has been said that it is impossible for man to look directly upon the face of God. Science has discovered that this is true. There is a theory in physics called “Heisenberg’s uncertainty principle” which states that we cannot measure precisely, at the same time, both the momentum and the position of a particle. In order to predict exactly what will happen within a given system, whether it be a thrown baseball or the weather, we have to know where it is and where it’s going. What Heisenburg’s uncertainty principle reveals is that we can know half, and only half, of the information required to predict what will happen in a system. The more we can know about the location of a sub-atomic particle, the less we can know about its momentum. The more we can know about the momentum of a sub-atomic particle, the less we can know about its location. This limit to our knowledge is not a result of our testing instruments being too crude or our equations not being precise enough, this limit to our knowledge is the way Reality is.

Knowledge can take us only so far. We can know as much as possible about something, and there will still be half of it that will remain unknown. In this way, the choices that we make in our Lives can be described as being governed precisely one half by free will, and one half by determinism.

This is, of course, the perfect equation. The essence of All is equally sameness and change, equally knowable and unknowable. And thank goodness it is this way. If All could be known, we would know exactly what was going to happen for all of eternity. How boring would *that* be? If Nothing could be known, we wouldn't have any idea at all what was going to happen at any given moment. How terrifying would *that* be?

There cannot exist only sameness or only change. There can only exist **THUS**, which is samenesschange. Maybe "samege" is a good word for It.

Me: Half, half, half. Is everything half this and that, half right and wrong?

Myself: All is whole and complete. When we put the All into conceptual form, the *concept* is less than complete.

Every thing, every event, every being, that is seen from a certain perspective can also be seen from another perspective. When you formulate your particular perspective into a concept (using your thought processes, or intellect) and then hold that concept to be the Truth, you are seeing only the "right" aspect of the concept that you have formulated. Every being in the universe has had a different and unique experience of Reality than every other being in the universe. Are the concepts that they have formulated from their particular perspective "wrong" just because they happen to differ from yours?

The words "right" and "wrong" do a very ineffective job of describing anything. They do not apply at all to Reality Itself, and they don't work very well for concepts either. They might work alright for mathematics, but for anything subjective, they suck. A good word to use to describe concepts about Reality is "ambiguous." "Ambiguous" means: "capable of two or more interpretations." Ya, that works really well.

Me: It's hard to accept that there is no such thing as right and wrong when it seems like there is so much that is wrong in the world and in my life.

Myself: Ya, life can be tough sometimes, but if we live it whole heartedly, it can also be wonderful. In fact I believe that existence *is* inherently wonderful and that we *make* it tough.

Me: Starvation is wonderful? War is wonderful? Pain is wonderful?

Myself: When one fully engages every experience in one's life, everything is wonderful. I know this is hard to understand, but when one stops trying to understand and just lets go, all that is left is wonder. When one lets go of running *away* from this and running *after* that; when one fully embraces the present, one can finally be at peace in **every** circumstance. There is nowhere to run to anyway. Can you be anywhere else but where you are? Can you be anyone else but who you are? Can you do anything else besides what you are doing? It all really becomes so clear when you see this for yourself.

Me: So I'm just supposed to mindlessly accept everything that comes my way? Let me ask you something.

Myself: Sure.

Me: When you get a bad headache, do you take any pain killers?

Myself: Yes, I usually do.

Me: Why? Isn't pain just as wonderful as no pain? If you live what you preach wouldn't you just be happy that you were in pain and continue on in your state of blissfulness? If you take pain killers, aren't you running away?

Myself: Good one. The problem here is not giving the correct answer, but rather asking the correct question.

Me: You're sidestepping! Come on smarty pants, I thought you were better than that.

Myself: Hey, give me a chance here before you jump

down my throat. The real challenge in (of) Life is not figuring out *what* to do, but rather *how* to do it. When I get a headache, the question is not: "should I take a pain killer or not?" the question is: "**am I fully engaged in whatever action I take**?" When one is fully engaged in all that one does, there is never any doubt what to do, you just do it.

Me: What does "fully engaged" mean?

Myself: Being present; having no separation between body and mind. Doing exactly what you are thinking and thinking exactly what you are doing.

Me: And when fully engaged there is no doubt as to what to do?

Myself: Right.

Me: So if a fully engaged person were to get a headache and the thought came into their head: "maybe I should take an Aspirin," they wouldn't question that thought at all, they would just go ahead and do it? If I did the first thing that popped into my head all the time I'd be in jail!

Myself: A fully engaged person doesn't do the first thing that pops into their head, a fully engaged person doesn't *have* any thoughts popping into their head.

Me: What do you mean?

Myself: A fully engaged (enlightened) person has perfect harmony of mind and body, which means that the body reacts instantaneously and spontaneously to the information given to it by the mind. In other words, mind and body are one.

Me: And aren't our thoughts the vehicle trough which our mind gives us this information?

Myself: No, our thoughts are our attempt at processing the information that our mind gives us.

Me: Well don't we need to process this information in order to make sense of it all? Don't we need to put it into some sort of order?

Myself: Nope.

Me: What do you mean "nope?" We should just wander around bumping into things, not knowing or understanding anything? Are you nuts?

Myself: The only thing that we really need to know is that the universe is perfectly ordered, and being that we *are*, and are *a part* of, the universe, we are also perfectly ordered. We don't need to understand what a tree is, or where it came from, or why it's there in order to keep from bumping into it. When you know, you understand that you don't have to understand.

Me: If everything is perfectly ordered, why is there so much pain and suffering in the world?

Myself: Pain and suffering arise when we lose our focus on Reality. When we lose our focus on Reality, it appears as though things in Life are unbalanced and then we try to regain this balance. Although well intended, this "trying" is ultimately futile and literally a waste of energy because Reality is already perfectly balanced. This doesn't mean that things shouldn't change, it just means that we can change without going through the pain and suffering that usually go along with change.

"Do unto others as you would have them do unto you." "Every action has an equal and opposite reaction." "Love your neighbour as yourself." "$E=mc^2$." These Spiritual teachings and scientific equations all speak of the perfect symmetry and unity that is existence. This is the way It is. This is the way we are. **We don't need to try to be what we already are**. To do so is to bring pain and suffering into your Life.

Me: All we have to do to rid the world of pain and suffering is just pay attention?

Myself: Yes.

Me: Pay attention to what?

Myself: To everything.

Me: Could you maybe narrow that down a bit for me?

Myself: Pay attention to what you are doing. When you pay attention to what you are doing, your body and your mind begin working in greater harmony, and doubt, confusion, and fear begin to disappear. When doubt, confusion, and fear begin to disappear, so will your pain and suffering.

Me: I'm finding it very hard to believe that all we have to do is pay attention to what we are doing and somehow that will magically solve all of Life's problems.

Myself: That's what faith is all about. We need to have faith that we know what to do without trying to figure out what to do. In order to heal the separation between mind and body, we must let go of the *illusion* that they are separate. This "letting go" is faith in action.

Me: What are we letting go of?

Myself: We are letting go of trying.

Me: Trying to do what?

Myself: Trying to do the right thing, trying to control things, trying to figure everything out.

Me: So we should just give up.

Myself: We should give up on trying.

Me: If I give up on trying, how on earth am I ever going to get anything accomplished?

Myself: "Trying" to do things is like trying to beat your heart. Your heart knows what to do and so do you. You don't have to try to live your Life any more than you need to try to beat your heart. Like the great sage Yoda said: "Do or do not; there is no try."

Can you ever not do what you are doing?

Me: What?

Myself: Think about this. *Can you ever* ***not*** *do what you are doing?*

Me: Yes, I have the choice to do something other than what I am doing. Right now I'm talking to you, but I could stop talking to you and go have a nap.

Myself: You just lost your focus on Reality.

Me: *What?*

Myself: As soon as you think that there is something "other than" you are believing in an illusion. When you stop talking to me and go have a nap, you would not be doing what you *were* doing, but you are still doing what you are doing. We are **always** *not* doing what we *were* doing, or *will* do, and we are always doing what we are doing. It is possible to be yourself and it is possible to change. It is not possible to not be yourself. Concepts of "other than" such as "that," "false," and "not," are what we use to describe the illusion; they do not apply to Reality. In Reality there is no such thing as "other than." Particle is not other than wave. Mind is not other than body. Tree is not other than seed. One thing is not other than everything.

Me: Okay, I get it. I can't say that I *understand* it, but I think (or don't think) I get it. Now that I get it, what do I do? I'm supposed to harmonize my body and mind, but exactly *how* do I do that? I know you've said things like "let go" and "pay attention," but what do those things mean in practical terms? How do I actually "let go" and "pay attention"?

Myself: Okay, I'll show you now. I'll show you **now**. Don't think about anything and just look around.

Me: Okay... Now what?

Myself: Why did you stop?

Me: I don't know. How long did you want me to do it for?

Myself: For as long as you could do it for.

Me: Well I didn't know that. Do you want me to do it again? I could definitely do it for longer if I tried.

Myself: Okay, sure.

Me: Okay, here I go... Well, how was that?

Myself: Fine.

Me: I did it for longer than the first time, didn't I?

Myself: Ya, I'm pretty sure you did.

Me: Well that was easy, but I didn't get much out of it.

Myself: What *did* you get out of it?

Me: Let's see… Nothing, really.

Myself: Perfect! Now you just have to learn to do that all the time.

Me: First of all, I don't think it's possible to live totally devoid of thoughts, and second of all, why would I even want to when I don't get anything out of it?

Myself: What did you expect to get out of it?

Me: I don't know. How about peace and happiness?

Myself: Do it again and then describe to me what you felt.

Me: Okay… Well I guess it was peaceful, but I'm not sure if I was exactly happy.

Myself: You were in that state for 11 seconds. Maybe if you were able to stay in that state longer and more often, you would experience more peace in your life. Maybe once you found your peace, you could realize your happiness.

Me: It's possible. But it's pretty hard to stay in that state. It doesn't seem to me that it would even be possible to remain like that all of the time. I think that there are times where we have to think.

Myself: You may be right. I'm certainly not at the place to say *exactly* what enlightenment is. What I *have* found though, is that the less I think *about* things and the more I think *on* things, the more peace I find, and the more peace I find, the more happy I am.

As far as being hard; ya, it's hard. In fact, enlightenment, being present, being Spiritual, whatever you want to call it, is **the hardest possible thing to do**. And yet, paradoxically, it is also the easiest thing to do.

Me: What do you mean?

Myself: Being present is the easiest thing to do right now, and it's the hardest thing to do all the time. At any given moment you can see things as they are without filtering them through your thoughts. However, to keep that focus without sliding back into your old programmed way of thinking is very difficult. It's kind of like climbing Mount Everest. Each individual step is very easy to take, but when you look at the whole journey, it looks very difficult.

It takes dedication and it takes practice. You may only be able to remain present for a short period of time when you start, but as you progress, that period of time will get longer and longer until, one day, you will always be present.

Me: This goes back to what you were saying earlier about Spiritual practice?

Myself: Exactly. The various Spiritual practices taught by different religions throughout the world all are ways in which the follower learns to harmonize mind and body. This is done by focusing one's attention directly on what you are doing to the point where thinking about what you are doing is no longer necessary. Whether it be reciting prayers, performing prostrations, beating yourself with a whip, or sitting peacefully in the lotus position, all of these rituals are designed to bring the participant to a place where mind and body have reached perfect harmony. From this state of perfect harmony one is free to focus directly upon the experience itself. The body is sort of put on automatic pilot where one no longer needs to tend to the flying of the plane and can simply sit back and enjoy the scenery.

This is why nearly all of the martial arts practiced on the planet today have Spiritual roots. Learning how to kick someone's ass can be just as Spiritual as saying your "Hail Marys" if you devote your total concentration to it.

The important part to realize is that **it doesn't matter *what* you do**. You could start up a religion with the main tenet being that the way to God was by standing on one leg while balancing a crystal on your head and chanting "wonka, wonka, wonka," and you'd be right.

Me: How on earth is standing on one leg while balancing a crystal on my head and chanting "wonka,

wonka, wonka," going to help me contact God?

Myself: You don't really *have to* contact God, you just have to realize that you *are* in contact with God. **God is not a being that requires accessing, God is the state of being itself**. Since we are always in a state of being, we are always in contact with God. What matters is whether or not we are paying attention.

If you stood on one leg while balancing a crystal on your head and chanted "wonka, wonka, wonka," and did so with perfect attention, you would be in contact with God; you would be one with your Spirit.

Me: You keep talking about attention, but I'm not really sure what you mean by it.

Myself: Have you ever been reading a book when suddenly you noticed that you couldn't remember anything about the last paragraph, and then you had to go back and read that part over again?

Me: Sure, lots of times.

Myself: That's attention. You could have sworn that you read every word in that paragraph, but when you try to recall what you just read, it comes up a blank. That's sort of what most of us are doing on a constant basis with our lives. It seems as though we are present and engaged in Life, but when we stop and take an honest look at ourselves, it feels like we're missing out on something.

Me: And what are we missing out on?

Myself: We are missing out on the experience.

Me: And by missing out on it, we have lost contact with our Spirit, with God?

Myself: In the bible, hell is described as separation from God. I would describe it more as separation *of* God rather than separation *from* God. God is a process and when we are doing something and thinking about something else, we have lost our focus on the whole of the process. After that, quite literally, all hell breaks loose.

When we lose our focus on the whole of the process, it appears as though the process itself is a bunch of separate pieces. We then try to take these separate pieces and put them back together in an attempt to once again create wholeness.

It's like we are taking the most exquisite painting ever created, cutting it up into a jigsaw puzzle and then trying to put it back together. The problem is that the jigsaw puzzle is only an illusion, the picture itself is whole and complete; it never actually split and therefore never needed to be put back together.

This brings us back to the very start of the book. When I asked you to describe yourself according to the "how," "who," "what," "where," and "when," questions, I was asking you to tell me what piece of the puzzle you were. When we cut up the picture, we need to assign ourselves to a piece so that we fit in somewhere. This piece of the puzzle that we assign ourselves to is our ego. Our ego is this separate piece that we are trying to fit in with the rest of the puzzle.

We don't want to be separate, we want to fit in, and from our ego's point of view, we have to either mold ourselves to fit the universe, or mold the universe to fit ourselves. Controllers are trying to fit in by moulding the universe to fit themselves, and controlees are trying to fit in by moulding themselves to fit the universe. We usually label flamboyant, outgoing, attention-seeking people as having big egos, but quiet, submissive, giving people may have just as many ego issues as the attention-seekers. Either way, neither of them are truly being themselves; they are trying to be who they tell themselves they should be, or they are trying to be who others tell them they should be.

It is impossible for the universe to mould itself into the shape you think It has to in order for you to fit in. It is impossible for you to mould yourself into the shape you think you have to in order to fit in to the universe. It's impossible to fit in at all because you're already in. You are in, you always were in, and you always will be in. The entire concept of an ego, of an identity separate from the rest of everything else is an illusion. God accepts you fully and totally as you are. When you find that quiet, peaceful centre within yourself; that ***is*** yourself, you will feel this acceptance.

Me: You're talking about forgiveness?

Myself: It goes even beyond forgiveness. It's pure Love. In the same way that wisdom transcends levels of intelligence, Love transcends levels of forgiveness. If forgiveness has conditions placed upon it (such as "I'll forgive you to a point"), then we must always be searching to attain the highest level of forgiveness (the "still forgived" section). But to place levels on forgiveness means that there is something beyond forgiveness itself. Love is beyond this forgiveness. It is forgiveness before forgiveness is even asked for. It transcends the concept of forgiveness altogether. True forgiveness has no bounds or limits. This true forgiveness of no bounds or limits is Love.

Me: You haven't talked much about Love so far. Isn't Love the basic tenet of most religions? Where does Love fit in with the harmonizing of body and mind?

Myself: Love is the manifestation of enlightenment through our actions. Let's take Jesus as an example. Jesus was an enlightened being and His enlightenment was revealed through His actions. Jesus reacted to everyone He met with compassion and acceptance. It's important to see, however, that He also felt rage and sadness at times. Love itself is not a single emotion apart from other emotions like hatred, envy, fear, joy, and sadness. Love is the carrier of these emotions. In a way, Love is all emotions at once.

Me: Explain.

Myself: God has been described as Love. God has also been described as light. Light is not a certain colour, nor is it the lack of colour; light is the state of all colours existing harmoniously as one. Love is not a certain emotion, nor is it the lack of emotion; Love is the state of all emotions existing harmoniously as one.

When we shine light through a prism, the colours within that light are revealed in the resulting spectrum. When we shine Love through a person, the emotions within that Love are revealed in the actions of that person. We have even assigned specific colours to represent different emotions, such as red for anger, green for envy, yellow for fear, and blue for sadness.

Whenever we feel the different emotions that we experience throughout our Lives, we must realize that they are merely the many aspects of Love manifesting itself through us. Whenever we feel angry at someone or whenever we feel afraid, we can look at it as just one of the many beautiful aspects of Love. When we act from our emotions, we are focusing on just one part of the whole, which is Love. When we see these emotions as parts of the whole, when they arise, we can look at them, feel them, and then act from a state of wholeness; we can act out of Love. When we act out of Love we can accept people as they are because we see them as pure light, pure love, rather than the individual colours or emotions that may manifest at times.

When we accept people as they are, they no longer need to *try* to fit in through the projection of the ego. When one no longer feels as though they need to project an ego, the energy that went into the projection of that ego can go directly into Life itself. When we Love and accept people for who they are, they won't feel any pressure to be anything but who they really are.

The same principle applies to yourself. When you see your whole self, who you *really* are, you will no longer feel the need to *try* to fit in because you will see that you never did *not* fit in. To exist is to fit in. It is so utterly and blatantly obvious that you fit in. If the universe didn't accept you, how could you exist?

Other peoples' thoughts *about* you are not you. Everything that you are and everything that you do in your Life is an expression of the total and complete acceptance of you by the universe. Be who you are and do what you do, there is nothing other than this.

The most important thing in Life is to experience **everything** to its fullest. Look directly upon the majesty and wonder of everything. Feel each and every emotion to its very core. Turn your eyes from nothing and open your heart to everyone. Your highest calling in this Life is to experience All that is given to you. Once you learn to Love and accept everything and everyone in your Life, everything else will fall into place.

Me: What do you mean by: "everything else will fall into place"?

Myself: You won't have any more problems.

Me: Everything will go my way?

Myself: More like you will be going everything's way. When you and everything are going the same way, you won't have to push against anything in order to get where you're going.

Me: That does sound easier, doesn't it? When I go

everything's way, I will live a good Life?

Myself: When you and everything are in harmony, you will live a perfect Life.

Me: Sounds like you're talking about Heaven.

Myself: If that's what you'd like to call it, sure.

Me: We get to Heaven through Love and acceptance?

Myself: Yes, and when we see people and things as they are, we will naturally Love and accept All.

Me: You're implying that we are already in Heaven.

Myself: Absolutely.

Me: *This* is Heaven? I don't think so.

Myself: You don't *think* so, hey? Why not?

Me: Well, I don't know about you, but I can see a few problems here on earth.

Myself: What are some of these problems?

Me: War, starvation, repression of freedom of speech and religion, the damage being done to the environment, to name a few.

Myself: You're right, there are a lot of problems out

there.

Me: So how can this be Heaven when all of these problems exist?

Myself: **When you realize Nirvana, Heaven will be**.

Me: What do you mean?

Myself: It does no good to live in Heaven without also possessing the correct state of mind. Even if we lived in a Heaven where everyone had plenty of food, were free from disease and death, and had freedom of speech, we still wouldn't be happy if we didn't possess the correct state of mind.

Me: Sounds pretty good to me. Why wouldn't I be happy in a place like that?

Myself: You already live in a place like that.

Me: No, I live in Canada.

Myself: Do you have enough to eat?

Me: Are you kidding, I have *too much* to eat!

Myself: Does anyone shoot at you?

Me: No.

Myself: Do you have the freedom to say what you want

and practice whatever religion you want?

Me: Pretty much.

Myself: Sounds like Heaven to me. It would probably sound like Heaven to about 90% of the world's population too. So why aren't you in a state of constant bliss?

Me: Because I feel like there's more.

Myself: You're right, there is more. There's more pleasure to run to and there's more pain to run from. There are more things to possess and more things to do. Wanting "more" is possessing the incorrect state of mind.

I'm going to tell you something that will be **very** hard to accept, but once you do, I mean really grasp the full meaning of what it implies, you will look at Life a lot differently.

It is a scientific certainty that space is infinite. When I say that it is a certainty, I mean that science is about as certain that space is infinite as it is that the earth is round. This means that our universe of 100,000,000,000 galaxies, each made up of 100,000,000,000 stars, is only one of infinite universes. Space is infinite. Time is infinite.

WE HAVE AN INFINITE AMOUNT OF THINGS TO DO AND AN INFINITE AMOUNT OF TIME IN WHICH TO DO THEM.

So where does this leave the concept of "more?" We already have infinity at our disposal, so where else is there to go? It is a lesson in futility to want more of infinity. Wanting more of what you already have, and what you can always have more of, is the very definition of unfulfillment. Again, this is very much like the person who longs to get to the horizon. Wanting more of what you already have and can always have more of is like wanting to walk to the horizon. The horizon extends for infinity in front of you, and yet is impossible to reach, so if you want something to chase, "more" should keep you busy for a while.

An enlightened person doesn't want to get to the horizon because he realizes that he *is already standing* on the horizon. Everyone is standing on the horizon, we just have to realize that we are and stop chasing what we can't help but always have. We are all enlightened, we just have to realize that we are.

Me: So we might as well all shrug our shoulders, sit down and just BE.

Myself: Sure.

Me: Sure?

Myself: If that's what you do, that's what you do.

Me: Once someone becomes enlightened, there's nothing else for her to do?

Myself: There's *everything* for her to do, but there's

nothing *else* for her to do.

Me: I just *love* it when you talk like that!

Myself: There is nothing else for us to do other than what we do. People sit down and people walk. Enlightened people sit down and enlightened people walk. A person walking to get to the horizon is walking and an enlightened person walking is also walking. The difference is that the person who is walking to get to the horizon thinks that when he gets there, he will be happy, and the enlightened person is happy just walking.

Me: People can be happy no matter where they are?

Myself: I believe so, yes.

Me: A person who is dying of starvation can be happy? A person who is being molested by their father can be happy? How can a person who is experiencing physical or emotional torment possibly be in a state of continual happiness?

Myself: It is very difficult. Realizing your enlightenment in every situation is the hardest possible thing in Life to do. Given this fact, once accomplished, it is also the most rewarding thing you can possibly do.

Perhaps "happiness" is not the best word here because "happiness" carries with it a strong emotional connotation. Perhaps the words "peace" or "contentment" would be better used here. Underlying everything that we think and feel, there is an eternal, ever-present state of peace and contentment. This state is realized when we realize our enlightenment.

Learning to ride a bike is hard for a child to do, but once mastered, riding your bike is one of the greatest joys in a child's life. During the learning process, there will be the inevitable scrapes and bruises, but eventually the child will learn. If the child never lets go of her desire to learn to ride a bike, it *will* come to fruition. It doesn't matter if the child's parents tell her that she will never learn to ride it, or if the neighbor kid pushes her off every time he sees her. If her intention to ride her bike is unwavering, it will happen.

If, on the other hand, her parents encourage, guide, and teach her along the way, she will learn to ride her bike much faster. If no one pushes her off the bike, she will be able to develop her skill unimpeded, and with fewer bumps and bruises.

Enlightenment is much the same way. Certain conditions may make it easier for us to realize our enlightenment, but if our dedication to enlightenment is unwavering, the realization of our enlightenment is inevitable.

Me: Once enlightenment is achieved, all suffering ends?

Myself: I believe so, yes.

Me: You're not sure?

Myself: If I am speaking for my own experience, I can't

honestly share with you what enlightenment is like because I haven't fully realized my enlightenment. What I *can* tell you from my own experience is that when I pay attention, I am repaid with goodness.

Me: When you pay attention, only good things happen to you? It sounds to me that you're paying attention only to the good things that happen in your Life and rejecting all of the bad things. Denying the existence of anything wrong in your Life doesn't mean that there actually *is* nothing wrong in your Life. How do you expect to become a better person if you don't accept and then change the things that are wrong in your Life?

Myself: Roy, I would like to thank you for providing me the opportunity to practice patience.

Me: Hey, if I'm not getting it, maybe you could do a better job of explaining it to me.

Myself: You're right, I could be doing a better job, but I am trying, and so are you. If we both keep cooperating, we can't fail.

The changing of things that are wrong in your Life is a natural result of paying attention. There is no need to first distinguish what is wrong and then stop doing those things. Not only is there no need to do this, it is **impossible** to do this.

We all know that change in the physical world requires energy. If we want to get up off the couch (usually a "good" idea), it's going to take some energy. If we want to change the momentum of an N.F.L.

running back (usually a “bad” idea) it’s going to take some (a lot of) energy. Let’s say that change in the Spiritual world also takes energy; it certainly seems like a struggle at times. If we want to change the things that are wrong in our Life, it’s going to take some energy. The most efficient way to change these things is to devote as much energy as possible directly to the process. When we label things “good” or “bad” and then try to do the “good” things, we use up some of the energy that could have gone directly into the change itself. The most effective way to do good things is to let go of trying to do them and just let your Life flow naturally through you.

Me: You said quite a while back that Spiritual practice is really about learning how to *not* change. Which is it?

Myself: Our Spirit **IS** as It observes change and sameness. Energy never changes, and yet is constantly changing form.

Me: “The more things change, the more they stay the same”?

Myself: Sort of like that. Like a sunset, a person on the Spiritual journey changes, but in such a way that it is imperceptible. The change takes place right in front of everybody’s eyes, but be darned if anyone can point out how this change came about or what it is exactly that has changed.

There is sameness; there is a sunset. There is change; the sunset changes. In the end, it doesn’t matter if we understand what or why the sunset is, what matters is that it's there to experience.

Me: Well I'm glad you said that in the end it doesn't matter if we understand because I'm pretty sure that I don't. Listen to me! I'm not even sure that I don't understand!

Myself: You don't have to understand with your head, you just have to be willing in your heart.

Me: How do I start?

Myself: Remember when I got you to not think and look around?

Me: Yep.

Myself: That is what we are going to practice. We will learn to do away with extraneous thought. More specifically, we will learn to pay attention, and as a result of our attentiveness, extraneous thought will not occur.

Me: …I quit.

Myself: No, you don't.

Me: Okay, I don't. But I have my doubts about this.

Myself: You can't expect to be a master right off the start. As with anything, when you start off learning something new, you're going to really suck at it.

Me: Jee, thanks for the words of encouragement!

Myself: Can you ride a bike?

Me: Everyone can ride a bike.

Myself: Everyone can realize their enlightenment. Just like learning to ride your bike took practice, so will learning to realize your enlightenment. Some children take longer than other children to learn to ride their bike, and some people will take longer to learn to realize their enlightenment. It just takes practice.

A professional athlete has put in countless hours practicing his sport in order to get to that level, and continues to practice in order to play at his best. When we engage in Spiritual practice, we are practicing how to play our best at Life Itself, so when we look at it this way, Spiritual practice is not really apart from anything else that we do. We can't practice being Spiritual while living any more than we can practice being wet while swimming.

None the less, as the saying goes "practice makes perfect," (maybe "with practice perfection is realized" works better here, but that's pretty long to be a catch phrase) so it is good to set aside a time each day to devote wholeheartedly the harmonizing of your body and mind. The easiest way in which to achieve this harmony is to simply sit in a comfortable manner in a quiet and still environment, close your eyes, and still your mind. A still body does not distract the mind and a still mind does not distract the body.

Do not try to stop your thoughts, but rather just observe them and let them run their course. If you find yourself grabbing onto your thoughts and running with them, just let them go again. Keep doing this as many times as you find yourself losing focus. Remember that when you start thinking *about* things, you have lost focus. When you think *on* things, you are focused. When your focus is on your thoughts, you are dealing with your concepts *about* Reality. When you are focused on Reality and no thoughts arise, you are dealing *with* Reality.

Me: How long should I do this for?

Myself: As long as you feel you should do it for. Just let your thoughts and actions happen without any attempt to control them or stop them. Quite often it is beneficial to focus on your breathing as a way to let go of your thoughts. When you feel that it is time to get up, it is time to get up. Do not fight against your thoughts or try to do anything with your thoughts. Just simply **be** and **observe**.

It is important to let your thoughts come and go of their own accord. Remember that all of existence is perfectly balanced and that any attempt to balance It is counter productive. If you drop a stone into a still lake, it will make waves. That's fine. The waves will become still of their own accord. Any attempt to "help" the waves become still will only cause more waves.

Me: If I "let my thoughts and actions happen without

any attempt to control or stop them" all of the time, what the heck is going to stop me from doing terribly evil things?

Myself: What makes you think you would do terribly evil things?

Me: Well if there is nothing there to control my thoughts and actions, I could do anything I wanted.

Myself: That sounds like freedom to me. Wouldn't that be a good thing?

Me: What if I wanted to rape, steal, and murder?

Myself: Have you ever wanted to staple your eyelids to your eyes?

Me: Can't say as I have.

Myself: Why not?

Me: For some reason it's just never crossed my mind.

Myself: Would it be safe to say that if the thoughts of rape, stealing, and murder never crossed your mind, you'd never want to do those things either?

Me: I suppose so, but then wouldn't it also follow that if the thoughts of Love and compassion never crossed my mind, I'd never want to do those things either.

Myself: If all you want is to be present, Love and compassion will naturally and effortlessly flow from you. If all you want is to be present, you don't need anything other than what you have, so you can give it all away. When one is entirely focused on the experience of the present, one experience is just as wonderful (full of wonder) as the next. If not having sex is just as wonderful as having sex, why rape anyone? If not owning a fancy car is just as wonderful as owning a fancy car, why steal one? If my Life is as wonderful as his, and if his is as wonderful and as valuable as mine, why take his?

Me: If drinking kool-aid is just as wonderful as drinking a fine wine, why drink the fine wine? You can't tell me that kool-aid tastes just as good as fine wine.

Myself: Fine wine and kool-aid taste different. One may describe one as tasting better than the other, but to an enlightened person the *experience* of tasting the one is just as "good" as the *experience* of tasting the other one.

When one focuses on the experience itself rather than the description of the experience, (the) All experience turns out to be "good." Seeing things as they are brings out the "best" of everything. For example, if you were to experience both the wine as it is and the kool-aid as it is, the experience of the kool-aid would be as "good" as the experience of the wine, as opposed to the experience of wine being as "poor" as the experience of the kool-aid. If you were to see everyone as they truly are, without definition or bias, you would Love everyone equally. Your Love for the guy who just screwed you out of $10,000.00 in a business deal would equal the Love you have for your child or your spouse. The Love you feel for the crook would go "up" to the Love you feel for your child.

When God created the universe, He described It as "good." "Good" is Reality's inherent nature. To experience Realty in its inherent state is to experience All as "good."

Me: If everything is just as good as everything else, why do we do one thing instead of another? If a pit bull chewing on my leg is just as good as it not chewing on my leg, why would I try to make it stop chewing on my leg?

Myself: We don't need a motivation to live our Life other than Life itself. The goal of Life is not to chase after pleasure and run from pain, the goal of Life is to just be happy.

Pleasure and pain flow along one's Life as naturally as a river flows down a hill. A river flows around the boulder and wears away the sandy ground. It does this naturally. We *could* try to explain it's behaviour in terms such as "choice," or "force" or "better", but "naturally" seems to sit most comfortably.

It would be quite natural to try to make the pit bull stop chewing on your leg. It would be quite unnatural to worry about the possibility of pit bulls chewing on your leg, or to keep reliving the experience of the pit bull chewing on your leg. When we talk of enlightenment or of Spiritual Life, what we are talking about is simply doing what comes about naturally. When you walk, the act of walking comes naturally. There is no need to "think" about how to lift up your left leg, move it forward, and then put it down, then lift up your right leg, move it forward, and then put it down. When your body is in perfect harmony with the universe, there is no need to "think" about anything that you do in your Life any more than you have to "think" about walking. When you are operating from Spirit, your entire Life becomes as natural and effortless as walking.

Me: Aren't there times where one is required to think? In this day and age where so much information is being transferred, don't I need to be able to process this information in order to function on a day-to-day basis? If everybody just suddenly stopped thinking altogether, our entire society would fall into chaos.

Myself: Think when thinking is necessary. What one needs to think upon, one should think upon. What one does not need to think upon, one need not think upon. What we are doing when we pay attention and act from Spirit, is we are doing away with extraneous thought. That is all.

Whatever you do, do it with attention. When you are doing your job, do your job with attention. When you are cooking supper (and while eating it), cook it (and eat it) with attention. When you are with your family, give your family your full attention.

You will do your job better, and you will enjoy your job more. You will eat healthier suppers, and they will taste better. You will be a better father and husband, and your whole family will be healthier and happier.

Me: You make it sound so easy.

Myself: **Living Life from Spirit is absolutely effortless. The *process of learning* to live Life from Spirit is the nearest thing to impossible that is still possible.**

Me: Are you sure it's possible?

Myself: Yes, I'm sure.

Me: How do you know for sure?

Myself: I don't know for sure.

Me: You just said that you were sure that enlightenment was possible and then you said that you didn't know for sure whether enlightenment was possible.

Myself: I know that I have faith that enlightenment is possible.

Me: Why can't you ever just answer a question directly? Why do you play these silly little word games?

Myself: Why do you keep asking questions?

Me: If I stop asking questions, how am I supposed to learn anything?

Myself: What is it that you wish to learn?

Me: I want to learn how to be enlightened.

Myself: You will be enlightened when you learn how to perfectly

kick a small stone

Me: You're getting all Zen on me aren't you?

Myself: Can't get anything past you can I?

Me: Nope, I'm pretty smart.

Myself: Are you smart enough to Love someone?

Me: What does how smart I am have to do with Loving someone?

Myself: Exactly.

Me: What does kicking a small stone have to do with Loving someone?

Myself: If you kick a *big* stone you'll stub your toe.

Me: You've totally lost me.

Myself: You do not exist as a separate entity that interacts with other separate entities; you are a part of a seamless continuum of infinite relationships. When you give your undivided attention to this relationship with (of) All, you will find wonder in small stones, big stones, and people. Each one of these relationships will be different (you might kick small stones, you probably won't kick big stones, you probably shouldn't kick people), but the feelings that accompany each relationship will be wonder and Love.

Me: Why would wonder and Love magically appear

just by paying attention? It sounds like you're over simplifying the whole process.

Myself: When I say that you are a part of a continuum of infinite relationships, I mean it literally. Henry Stapp, a physicist at the Lawrence Berkeley Laboratory in California during the 1970's described the physical world according to quantum physics as: "… not a structure built out of independently existing unanalyzable entities, but rather a web of relationships between elements whose meanings arise wholly from their relationships to the whole." K.C. Cole, a teacher at UCLA writes in her book *The Hole In The Universe* the following: "like the birds and fish of an Esher woodcut, something and nothing can't be teased out, one from the other, to stand as separate entities unto themselves.[1] The universe is just one big happy tapestry of tangled relationships that can never be unraveled. There is no chair here, butterfly there; particle here, void there; time here, gravity there. There is only the picture that emerges from all pulling together, a great mosaic that seems unrecognizable close up, but comes into focus as we stand back and observe from a more distant, and broader, perspective."

There is no "me" without a relationship with "you." There is no "you" without a relationship with "me." "You" are an equally important part of the process of the relationship as "me." "Me" is the body (one "thing") aspect of the *relationship* that is the real me, and "you" (everything "else") is the mind aspect of

---

[1] It is interesting that Buddha said "Form is emptiness, emptiness is form" ***2500*** years ago. Maybe he knew a bit about Reality…

the *relationship* that is the real me. The Real me, the harmonious relationship of my body and mind, is Spirit.

"Do unto others as you would have them do unto you," and "Love your neighbor as yourself" resound with so much truth because others *are* you and your neighbor *is* yourself. When you see Reality as It is, you see that others are just as much a part of you as your body. As a result it is as natural to care to another's suffering as it is for you to care to an open gash on your arm.

Me: What about wonder? It's not very wonderful to have an open gash on your arm.

Myself: When your mind and body are one and you are living from Spirit, you see things and understand things at a deeper level. Let me give you an example. Look at these two objects:

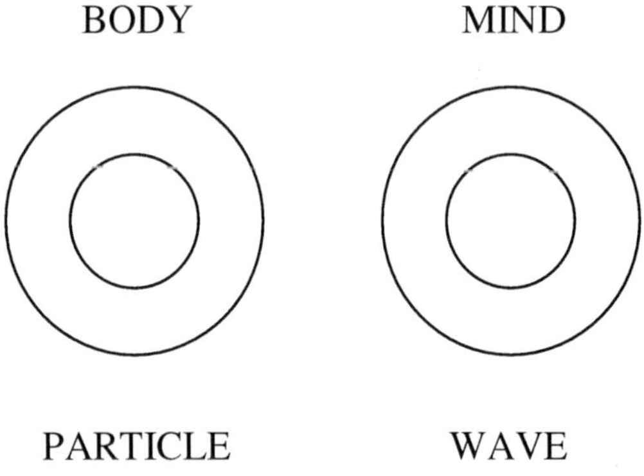

You will see that I have labeled one "body" and "particle," and the other "mind," and "wave." These two symbols represent how we see the world when we believe that our bodies are separate from the rest of the universe. Looks normal enough, doesn't it?

Me: I can't see anything wrong with it.

Myself: There is nothing wrong with it, except that it could be experienced at a deeper level.

Me: How?

Myself: Look at them again, but this time focus your eyes so that each of the images break into two and then superimpose one image over the other. It may take a little practice, but when you get the hang of it the resulting image will come in clear and you will be able to focus on it and look at it without effort.

Me: ...Yes... I got it! Wow! When I focused on the superimposed image it somehow looked larger and three dimensional. It just jumped off the page.

Myself: This is how things look when one is living from Spirit. When body becomes harmonized with mind, everything just seems to pop out and All becomes much more interesting and wonderful. You see and understand Reality at a deeper level. This is Spirit. When we were simply looking at body and mind as separately existing entities, Spirit was nowhere to be found. Indeed, Spirit is invisible and undetectable when one accepts that body and mind are separate. Spirit is only revealed through the harmonizing of body and mind, at which time It becomes more Real than the "reality" that existed as a separate mind and body.

When your focus is on Spirit, body and mind do not disappear, but rather they remain at the periphery where their illusionary nature is revealed. Your Life's focus is no longer on body or mind because, quite frankly, they're boring compared to your Spiritual Life.

Me: Yes, I see what you mean. I literally see what you mean. I can also see that the labels of "body" and "mind," and "particle" and "wave" become nonsensical when one is focused on Spirit.

Myself: Right. It doesn't make any sense that a particle can also be a wave or that you can also be the entire universe, and therefore all attempts at defining such a state become impossible. Spirit is indefinable, and when we split It up we can define It; or when we define It, we split It up.

So let's go back to the gash on your arm. When you are directly experiencing Reality, there really is nothing but wonder. A gash on your arm is as full of wonder as an orgasm when you focus on the experience. You may feel pain beyond description and you may feel pleasure beyond description. When you are operating from the perspective of Spirit, you experience All of your Life from a level that is beyond description. Tying your shoe is beyond description. Stubbing your toe is beyond description. Watching your children play is beyond description. **When you stop**

labeling things, All that is left is wonder.

This does not mean that everything becomes the same. Every experience throughout ones Life is different, and every experience is wonderful. In this way, ones Life becomes entirely engrossing and spontaneous. There is no need to seek out pleasure and avoid pain because All arises and passes away naturally. There is pleasure and there is pain, there is happiness in it All.

Me: How can I be happy when I'm in pain?

Myself: How can you be happy when you're in pleasure?

Me: I've never really thought about it before. I just seem to naturally be happy when I'm experiencing pleasure.

Myself: You are happy when you experience pleasure because you don't want to be somewhere other than where you are. You are unhappy when you experience pain because you want to be somewhere other than where you are. Problems (usually in the form of addiction) arise when we associate pleasure with happiness.

It is not the experience of pleasure or pain itself that causes happiness or suffering, it is your willingness or unwillingness to remain present and fully experience the pleasure or pain. Basically speaking, being present = happiness, not being present = suffering.

If you cut your arm, do what you must do to heal

the pain, but you shouldn't wish that it never happened or that it would go away. It *did* happen and it *will* go away (change). We must accept the things that happen and we must accept that the things that happen change. It is not our duty to make things happen or to make things change. That part is being taken care of; you don't have to worry about it. You don't have to worry about anything.

Me: But I want to make a difference. I want to change my life. I want to make the world a better place. I want to make my life better. You make it sound like nothing I do makes any difference. If that's true then what's the point in doing anything at all?

Myself: There *is* never, and *will* never be a time where you are not doing things. There is never and will never be a time where you are not changing things. With everything you think and everything you do you are changing things. The question is never whether you're making a difference or not, the question is…

Me: No, no, let me guess. The question is whether or not I'm paying attention.

Myself: You've been paying attention.

I know you want to be a better person, and that you want to help make the world a better place for other people, and that's great. What is the best way to do these things? How do we become better people and live happier Lives? We can quote wise sayings like, "love your neighbour as yourself" and try to adhere to written rules like the Ten Commandments for eternity, but how do we actually ***do*** these things?

If we actually see our neighbor as our self, we won't have to try to Love him as our self. If you see everything as It is, without separating things and labeling them, there will be no distinction between "you" and "them." When there is no distinction between "you" and "them," you will Love your neighbor as yourself because your neighbor *will* be yourself.

Me: You can talk 'till you're blue in the face (which you have, by the way) about how we're not separate, but we *are* separate. I'm here and you're there. There is space between us. Surely you can't dispute that!

Myself: We're both here, aren't we?

Me: We're both here in one way, but I'm here and you're there in another way.

Myself: Our mind is here, our bodies are here and there. "Here" is a description relative to the boundary conditions that we place upon the whole. The "here" that you are calling yourself is merely a description of the boundary condition of your skin. If you were to expand the boundary condition to the walls of this room, we would both be "here." If you were to expand the boundary condition to the planet earth there would be 6+ billion of us "here." If we expand the boundary condition to include the entire universe, we are all "here." From the perspective of a skin cell inside your body, it would be "here" and the skin cell next to it would be "there" but they would both be "here" inside your body.

Me: I think that I'm picking up on an ongoing theme here; what things are is relative to the perspective taken.

Myself: How we describe things is relative to the perspective taken.

Me: If that's true, then there is no "Ultimate Reality."

Myself: There is an "Ultimate Reality," but It is neither subjective nor is It objective. Ultimate Reality is equal part subjective *and* objective. From our subjectiveness arise our objects. Just as we divide the earth's land mass and bodies of water into different countries and oceans, so do we divide Reality into you and me. Although it's hard to accept, the lines that we draw that separate you and me are just as arbitrary as the borders that we draw up that separate one country from the next. In Reality there are no lines suddenly appearing on the ground telling us that one part of the earth is somehow different from the part right next to it. When we see things as being separate from other things, we are putting our own little subjective spin on Reality.

We constantly make the mistake of believing that *how* we see things is actually the way they are. Let's look at a glass of water with an ice cube floating in it. Looking at the process at arms length, it appears as though there is a definite (solid) object called an ice cube floating around in another, although less definite (liquid), object of water. However, if we were to look very closely at where the solid object of the ice cube meets with the liquid object of the water, we will find that it is impossible to identify where one object begins and the other object ends. If we look at the essence of the water itself - the water molecules - the liquid form of the water will have water molecules moving around more than the solid form of the water. However, there will be no definite line where one can say "this is where the ice cube ends and this is where the water begins." There will only be water molecules that are moving around less and water molecules that are moving around more. Even the apparent line where the water turns into air is nothing but a constant process of water molecules moving slower (the water in the glass) and water molecules moving faster (the water molecules that have evaporated into the air). The essence of each form of the water, from the solid ice cube to the liquid water to the gas water in the air, is the water molecule. With every water molecule we look at, there will invariably be another water molecule next to it that is moving a bit faster, and another water molecule next to it that is moving a bit slower. Exactly where one form stops and the other form starts is impossible to determine.

If we apply this same concept to you and me and trees and Volkswagen Beetles, what we find is that all things share the same essence. So when we look very closely at the line that divides you from the rest of the universe, namely your skin, we find the essence of you in your skin, but we also find that same essence in every single air molecule around your skin. We also find that same essence in me, in trees, and in Volkswagen Beetles. Exactly where one form stops and another form starts is impossible to determine. We are all different forms of the same essence.

Me: When did we lose it? What was it that caused us to lose sight of our true nature?

Myself: Well that's the story of the original sin that we read of in the bible. When Adam ate the fruit of the tree of conscience (con-science?), he was made aware of right and wrong, good and bad. The original sin turns out to be the original act of separation. The original sin was not murder, or stealing, or lying; it was the act of separation. Everything else that we've screwed up since then has been a result of the ongoing belief that things are separate. Murder, stealing, lying, and the like are a result of the belief in separateness.

Adam was kind of like a cancer cell. He was the first person of the human species that believed he was separate from the rest of the universe. He got his wires a bit crossed up and as a result he started doing things that were not part of his true nature. The same thing happens to a cell that becomes cancerous. The cell gets some bad information, usually from a part of its DNA getting knocked out of whack, and loses track of its true nature. The cell then starts consuming its host body and replicating uncontrollably. It no longer realizes that it is a part of a larger body and that its Life is dependant upon the Life of the host body. The cancer spreads throughout the body consuming more and more nutrients and energy as it spreads. Eventually the cancer has used up so much of the body's resources that the body dies and so does the cancer die with it.

Unfortunately, this description more accurately describes the human species than any other. We are acting on information that is causing us to get out of whack. Adam somehow received some bad information (from Satan, I guess) and that led to the belief that right is separate from wrong and the attempt to do right and not do wrong has led us to not acting in our true nature. We are a cancer on this host body we call Earth, and we are using up so much of its resources that it may lead to its, and as a result our own, death.

Me: Didn't you say a long time ago that everything was perfect?

Myself: That sounds like something I might say.

Me: If that's true then everything we do, even things that are not in our true nature, are perfect. So maybe not doing things in our true nature is in fact part of our true nature.

Myself: You've got me on that one!

Me: I do?

Myself: I agree that we are allowed to live our Life as we please and that there is no "wrong" way to live It. We will live. We will be born, live our Life, and then die. About that there is no question. The question is: will we live a happy, healthy, balanced Life, or will we live a fearful, unhealthy, unbalanced Life?

When you're fearful, you won't want to go anywhere because you're too scared. When you're unhealthy, you can't go anywhere because you're too sick. When you're unbalanced, you're too busy falling down to get anywhere. A life that is happy, healthy and balanced leads to a greater degree of freedom than one that is fearful, unhealthy, and unbalanced.

In nature there are no fences or walls or rules that inhibit our freedom. I guess that when I say something is our true nature, what I'm saying is that our true nature is whatever leads us to a greater degree of freedom.

Me: So our true nature is to be free?

Myself: Yes.

Me: And we get back to our true nature by…

Myself: Doing as nature does. Nature doesn't consume more than it needs. That's the big one. There is no such thing as an obese lion. A lion eats what it needs, that's all. When it dies, vultures and bugs will eat it and what isn't eaten will go back into the ground as nourishment for the grass. Everything is balanced in nature; the individual takes from its environment precisely what it needs, and the environment takes back exactly everything that the individual doesn't need. Humans act a bit differently.

Humans seem to take much more than they need and therefore the environment can't take back everything that the humans don't need. As a result, the waste piles up and the whole system becomes unhealthy. If we were to just pay attention to what the environment, other people, and even our own bodies are telling us, we would live a much more balanced and healthy Life.

We are becoming more and more distracted from what our mind is trying to tell us. We have games on our cell phones. We have DVD players in our cars. We watch countless hours of television. We have lost touch with our environment, with each other, and even with our own bodies. The result has been an environment that is losing its ability to sustain Life, the many atrocities that we as a species inflict upon each other, and a society here in North America where over half of the population is overweight.

All of these problems have arisen from the fact that we aren't paying attention. When we don't listen to what our bodies are telling us, we become unhealthy; it's that simple. We know what and how much to eat; our bodies are telling us these things if we only listen. If you are paying attention to your body, you will eat when you are hungry and you will stop eating when you are no longer hungry. Your body will be naturally fit and healthy when you are in touch with your body. The same goes for all of the relationships that you are a part of in your Life. If we as a species pay attention to the environment, our environment will be healthy. If you as an individual pay attention to the people in your Life, your relationships with those people will be healthy. The universe is telling us what to do to live harmoniously and happily. When your body and mind are working in harmony, "what to do" comes naturally and effortlessly. It is as if the universe is guiding you with flashing neon signs telling you which way to go and what to do. It really is that obvious when you pay attention.

But how can we pay attention to what our bodies are telling us when we are watching T.V.? How can we pay attention to what the environment is telling us when we are driving through it in our SUV's with the windows up and the stereo on? How can we pay attention to what our family, and our friends, and our neighbors, and people of different religious beliefs are telling us when we've got our own thoughts bouncing around in our heads? We need to slow down, shut up, and **PAY ATTENTION**. Turn off the television and have a quiet meal as a family. Get out and take a walk in nature. Visit your neighbor. Learn what other religions are **really** about.

Me: Speaking of religions, what *are* they really about and why is there so much fighting and disharmony between so many practitioners of different religions?

Myself: A religion is a guide to lead us to enlightenment based upon the Life and teachings of an enlightened person. Christianity is a guide to enlightenment based upon the Life and teachings of Christ. Buddhism is a guide to enlightenment based upon the Life and teachings of Buddha. The problem between religions is not with the guides, the problem is that some people think that the way their guide teaches is right and that the way other guides teach are wrong.

We all know that different people who share the same experience will naturally describe that experience differently. Two different people who make it to the summit of Mount Everest will relate their experience differently and it would be ridiculous to believe one persons' story to be "right" and the other persons' story to be "wrong." There can be no doubt that both climbers' stories will be very similar, but to expect them to tell the exact same story would be ludicrous. It would be impossible for two different climbers that made it to the top of Mount Everest at two different times on two different trails to tell the exact same story.

When Buddha and Christ (and all the other enlightened beings who have shared their experience with us) describe their experience of enlightenment in different terms, why do we (especially Christians) think that one description is "right" and the other description is "wrong?"

Two different biology teachers teaching the same course will undoubtedly teach their classes in two very different manners. Some students may prefer one teacher's methods over the others, but to say that one teacher's method is right and the other teacher's method is wrong would be silly.

Me: Well I don't know about Buddha, but Jesus said: "I am the way, the truth and the life, no man comes to the Father but through me."

Myself: Jesus spoke in parables all the time. Why do we choose to take this quote so literally? Christians' (miss) interpretation of this one small quote has done more to mess up the Christian religion than anything else.

Me: That quote seems pretty to-the-point to me. How could someone possibly misinterpret "I am the way, the truth and the life, no man comes to the Father but through me."?

Myself: Read this: "I am."

Me: I am.

Myself: Okay, I interpret that as you stating that you *are*. Now read it with the emphasis on the "I."

Me: *I* am.

Myself: Now I interpret that as you saying that *you* are. The inference would be that you are saying that *you* and only *you* exist. Even the simplest statement, especially a written statement, can be interpreted in different ways.

Me: Okay, so how do *you* interpret the statement: "I am the way the truth and the life, no man comes to the Father but through me"?

Myself: If we go back to the listing of the various triune systems that describe Reality, we will recall that Jesus was the physical, or body, aspect of the system, and the Holy Ghost was the mind aspect of the system. When Jesus said that no man can come to the Father except through himself, perhaps what he was saying was that we must find our Spirit through our physical Life. Through the experience of Reality through our physical Life we access God, for **God *is* the direct experience of Reality** through the harmony of our body and our mind. Jesus was a man that had perfect harmony of body and mind, and therefore he was able to directly experience Reality. Jesus and the Holy Ghost were in perfect communication and through that perfect communication, His Godliness was realized. That is why He could make the astonishing claim that He and God the Father were one and the same.

Me: So was Jesus the Son of God, or was He just a man?

Myself: Was Jesus a man?

Me: Yes.

Myself: Was He just an ordinary man?

Me: No.

Myself: Would you like to live like Jesus did?

Me: Yes.

Myself: Do you really need to know anything more than this?

Me: …I guess not. Not really.

Myself: That is good. You have asked a lot of questions and that is good. You may be beginning to realize that there is no end to questions, and that is *very* good.

Me: Yes, but somehow I get the feeling that out of all the questions that I've asked you so far, you haven't really *answered* even one of them.

Myself: The Spiritual journey isn't about finding definite answers, it's about finding balance in your Life. A question is nothing more than a scale used to weigh the options, and there are an infinite amount of answers perfectly balanced on both sides. Whatever you decide to label those sides; be it "yes" and "no," "right" and "wrong," "particle" and "wave," or "body" and "mind," you will always find that you can't have one without the other. Life's quest is not to do only the "right" things, it is to live a balanced Life. From that balanced Life, the right things will naturally be done.

Jesus said that the path that leads to Heaven is a "straight and narrow way." The straightest and narrowest way that I can think of is a tight rope.

Buddhism is often referred to as "the middle way." The way of the tightrope walker is the ultimate middle way.

Those of us on the Spiritual path are very much like tightrope walkers; we need to focus and pay attention with every step that we take in order to keep our balance.

Me: Is it all really worth it? Do we get anywhere, or do

we just keep walking on the tightrope forever? Where is the end to it all?

Myself: There is no end to existence, but there is an end to suffering. We *have* always existed and we *will* always exist. There is no end to existence. There are cycles that existence goes through, like birth and death, but Life is timeless and eternal. We will do all that that there is to do; and there is **no end** to the things we can do.

Will we go through eternity missing out on this wonderful experience of Life by simply not paying attention? Will we read the book, but not *really* read it?

Me: You're asking questions. I thought that we were getting to the point where we no longer needed to ask questions.

Myself: There you go trying to be funny again. A sense of humor is an important thing to have. When you realize that everything that you take so seriously and get so worked up about is nothing more than a creation of your own thinking mind, you will laugh.

Me: You're trivializing my fears and worries, aren't you?

Myself: No. All that you feel is valid. You must simply realize that your thoughts and feelings are not your whole and true self.

The next time you meditate, just watch your thoughts. Let them rise and fall of their own accord.

You will find that all of your fears and worries are nothing more than a product of your own thoughts. When you find your center, your source, the cares of your ego will fade into obscurity and there will be nothing left to fear and nothing left to worry about.

Your source is the part of you that is not just the things that exist within the cycle of existence; It is the cycle of existence Itself. You are not the things that happen *in* your Life; you are Life itself. Life cannot die. If it did, it would not be Life. There is Life, and Life is sameness and change.

Do you understand?

You cannot be other than Life. You *must be.* You must be you and you must do what you are doing. It must be this way because it *is* this way. Can there be another way other than the way there is? If you think that It shouldn't be this way, you cannot win. If you accept that It is this way, you cannot lose.

In one way, you cannot win. In one way, you cannot lose.

The choice is yours.

If you choose to live your Life thinking of ways to change things, you cannot win.

If you choose to live your Life with attention and with acceptance, you cannot lose.

Life is a game that we cannot lose, but in the trying to win It, we do not. Do you see? You cannot win at Life if you try to, and you cannot lose at Life if you accept It.

Every moment that we experience in our Life is there for a reason and should be treated with great reverence. You are the vehicle through which All of

Creation manifests.

Every thought that you have, every emotion and feeling, every other person and object that you share existence with is telling you a story. It is telling you the story of yourself. Listen.

Me: Wow. Is every moment in my life really that important?

Myself: Yes.

Me: That's pretty heavy. That seems like a lot of pressure to be under.

Myself: There's no pressure. Patience is just like forgiveness in that there are no restrictions on it. There are no limits placed upon your enlightenment. You can realize your enlightenment now or you can realize your enlightenment twenty seven lives from now. Your enlightenment will never leave you. It can't.

Me: Well that's reassuring. One more question.

Myself: Shoot.

Me: Who exactly are you and who the heck am I?

Myself: One of the most important questions one can ask is: "who am I." Any answer that you or anyone else can come up with to that question will only be your ego - a description of who you are in relation to certain circumstances that come up in the continuum of your

Life.

When you say "I am a husband" or "I am a mother" or "I am a Christian" or "I am an alcoholic," you can accept that description to be true on a certain level and then leave it at that level. Your whole, True, Spiritual self is utterly beyond description and completely transcends all levels, boundaries, and concepts that may be placed upon It. When we believe that the whole of what we are is the various descriptions of our ego, we restrict our Spiritual growth.

We cling to our egos like we cling to the face of a mountain in the belief that if we let go, we will fall to our death. We think that without a reference point for our identity, we will somehow simply cease to exist. In order to live our Life free of boundaries and free of fear, we must let go of our ego - who we *think* we are - and trust in our True self - who we Really are. When we totally and completely let go with total and complete faith, we will find that not only will we not fall to our death, but that all along we actually knew how to fly!

With nothing to hold onto anymore we are free to *be*, and to *do*, and to *experience* All. I'm not talking about experiencing a certain degree of freedom, I'm talking about experiencing freedom itself! In order to be totally and completely free, we cannot hold onto anything. Like a leaf that grows on the tree and then lets go to let the wind carry it where it will, we must let go of our Life and let the universe carry us where it will. A leaf "knows" where to land, and you know what to do. It's all right to let go. It will be scary at first, but it will be all right.

Me: Just let go.

Myself: Just let go.

Me: But you never answered who you were. Before I let go, I need to know who *you* are. If I'm a part of you, then I need to know who you are in order to know who I am.

Myself: You know who I am.

Me: I do?

Myself: You know everything. Well at least everything that you *need* to know.

Me: This is more of that funny thing that we were just talking about, right?

Myself: Well it *is* funny, but it's also true.

Me: But if I know everything, then why…

Myself: Shhh… It's alright. Remember what I told you?

Me: Which part?

Myself: The part where you felt your mind open. The part where you had an epiphany.

Me: How did you know about that?

Myself: It doesn't matter. What matters is that you now know what to do. **Knowing what to do is a major step in the Spiritual process. This is very important. <u>Now that you know what to do, you must put this knowledge into practice</u>.**

Me: So now all I have to do is to stay totally focused on Reality for the rest of eternity. *That* should be easy!

Myself: It *is* easy. It's the parts when you are not focused on Reality that are hard. Have patience. Remember that this is the hardest thing in all of existence to do. Remember that we have infinity to realize our enlightenment.

Would you get mad at a baby who hasn't yet learned how to walk?

Me: Of course not. Everyone must learn stuff like that on their own time; me getting mad won't help things.

Myself: Well then, do you think that it helps things if you get mad at yourself when you lose attention? Do you think that it helps things if you get mad at others when they lose their attention?

Me: I guess not.

Myself: When you find that you have lost your focus, regain it. That is all. When you find your self hanging onto your thoughts *about* Reality, let them go and **experience Reality directly. This is the way to liberation**.

Just keep coming back. Lose attention ten billion times, gain it back ten billion times. Love and accept yourself (by now you know that means others too) along the way. *NEVER QUIT.* **NEVER QUIT AND YOU CANNOT FAIL.**

Me: But…

Myself: **There is a point where no more talk is required. This is that point. Either you believe or you don't. If you do, then you know what to do and now you must do it. If you don't, then you must keep searching.** Either way, it's alright.

Me: *What's* alright?

Myself: One thing. Everything. All.

Me: How can you be so sure?

Myself: **Just look**. Do you see? **It's All Right.**

Me: Just look… Oh Yes, I see…

I…

MUSINGS

Our nervous system is an antenna used to receive the information that the universe is sending us. Our brains are the tuners. When we are thinking, we are trying to tune our brain onto the universes' frequency. Our thoughts are actually static. When you are thinking, you are listening to static. This is an indication that you have lost the universes' signal. When you get the right channel tuned back in, there is no more static.

* * * *

Even the most euphoric illusion is unsatisfying. Even the most horrific Reality is fulfilling.

* * * *

Believe my words to be false until you find my words to be true. Then you won't have to worry about my words being either false *or* true.

* * * *

"Why" is the most important question; I cannot speak of answers.

* * * *

Just as the smallest light cannot be dispelled by infinite darkness, the smallest *Reality cannot be dispelled by infinite +illusion.

*Truth and +delusion also work quite well, as does *Love and +hatred, and *Peace and +confusion.

Philosophy is the art of pointing out the obvious in the most complicated way possible.
Zen is the art of living a complicated Life in the most obvious way possible.

*   *   *   *

Spiritual atheism.

*   *   *   *

God can Love, accept, and forgive you only to the degree that you can Love, accept, and forgive yourself.

*   *   *   *

If you strike out on a journey and your path is straight and unwavering, the farthest possible distance travelled will invariably bring you back to your starting place.

*   *   *   *

We are all just as much to blame and not to blame for our mental illnesses as we are to blame and not to blame for our physical illnesses.

*   *   *   *

Life is made up of infinite moments of timelessness.

Q: Buddha, Einstein, and Freud are playing Texas Hold'em. Einstein knows the statistical probabilities of each and every hand, but can't read the other players. Freud can read the other players like a book, but doesn't know the statistical probabilities. Buddha is enlightened. What is the result?
A: They all break even but Buddha had the most fun watching the whole game take place.

* * * *

Reality trumps fantasy every hand.

* * * *

Most of us deceive ourselves not with delusions of grandeur, but rather with delusions of insignificance.

* * * *

Karma is the path of least resistance that we take to get back to our egos.

* * * *

Every fact requires a leap of faith to get to. Every leap of faith requires a fact to leap from.

* * * *

If you think that you are "here" and the universe is "out there," you are out of your mind.

We sacrifice happiness on the altar of pleasure on a daily basis.

* * * *

Being present is not a way to forget about your problems; it is the way to remember that you don't have any problems.

* * * *

The biggest lie that we tell ourselves is everything that we tell ourselves.

* * * *

Egos are masks pulled over the face of God.

* * * *

One cannot fully embrace the present while holding onto the past or grasping for the future.

* * * *

"Sooner or later it all gets real." – Neil Young.

Bibliography

Cole, K.C. *The Hole In The Universe.* San Diego: Harcourt,
2001

Greene, Brian. *The Fabric Of The Cosmos.* New York: Random
House, 2004.

Kaku, Michio. *Hyperspace.* New York: Doubleday, 1995.

Suggested Reading

How To Know God. Deepak Chopra. Harmony Books, 2000

The Dancing Wu Li Masters. Gary Zukav. Bantam Books,
1980.

Awareness. Osho. St. Martin's Griffin, 2001

No Boundary. Ken Wilber. Shambala, 2001

The Tao Of Physics. Fritjof Capra. Shambala, 2000

The Power Of Now. Eckhart Tolle. New World Library, 1999

The Fabric Of The Cosmos. Brian Greene. Knopf, 2004

Roy Dopson can be emailed at: roydop@sasktel.net